THE
SALLY
TRAFFIC
HANDBOOK

THE
SALLY
TRAFFIC
HANDBOOK

Facts, fun and frolics from
BBC Radio 2's Sally Boazman

Haynes Publishing

A catalogue record for this book is available from the British Library

ISBN 978 1 84425 461 3

Library of Congress catalog card no 2007935752

Published by Haynes Publishing, Sparkford, Yeovil, Somerset BA22 7JJ, UK
Tel: 01963 442030 Fax: 01963 440001
Int. tel: +44 1963 442030 Int. fax: +44 1963 440001
E-mail: sales@haynes.co.uk
Website: www.haynes.co.uk

Haynes North America Inc., 861 Lawrence Drive, Newbury Park,
California 91320, USA

Illustrations by Tim Bulmer (www.timbulmerartist.com)
All photographs courtesy Sally Boazman unless otherwise stated.

Designed and typeset by James Robertson

Printed and bound in Britain by J. H. Haynes & Co. Ltd, Sparkford

Contents

DEDICATION

This book is dedicated to my son, Harry, without whom nothing matters at all. And to my Mum and Dad, who would have loved all the fuss.

'I listen every day. My favourite shows are Wogan and Chris Evans. I really listen out for Sal's reports. To be honest, without them we'd all be lost. We wouldn't be able to divert and get away from it all. And it's thanks to the people who ring in. It works. Sally gives a damn, where a lot of people don't. Often people think of hauliers as the dregs of society, but Sally doesn't. She cares…and she also knows her way around, which helps. And her voice…absolutely fantastic.'
Frank Digman, from Cambridgeshire

Foreword

BY STEVE WRIGHT

When I first started my Afternoon Show on Radio 2 back in 1999, I didn't really want a traffic reporter at all. Up until then, I'd always read out the traffic news myself, and couldn't see any reason to change things. But Sally did change things. As soon as she started and I heard her delivery and style I knew I'd been wrong, and that everything would be OK.

What I really like is that she talks to drivers directly, on a one-to-one basis, and makes them feel part of a big club. It can't be much fun driving up and down the country day in and day out, and we all do our best at Radio 2 to make each day a bit special. But Sally is loved by every driver in the country because they know she looks out for them and speaks to each one as if they're the most important thing in the world. And I reckon that to her, they are.

One day her computer broke down and she couldn't print out her script so she walked into the studio with nothing in her hands. But you'd never have known it, because she had everything in her head, and unbelievably delivered a faultless report giving drivers across the country all the information they needed. Staggering. In my view she's not your average traffic reporter, but someone who has clearly become a bit of a national treasure.

It's no wonder that drivers all over the country have taken her to their hearts, and there's a few of us at Radio 2 who quite like her as well.

Oh, and she smells nice too.

FOREWORD

Introduction

When I began as Radio 2's first dedicated traffic reporter, a lot of people said that national traffic news just couldn't be done with any accuracy or authority. They were sceptical that one person could, in around two minutes, give a comprehensive picture of the state of the nation's roads. I took this on as a challenge, made a few rules for myself, and got started. One way or another it's worked out OK, but on my way to understanding what it is that drivers want, I've learned an awful lot. So I thought I'd share some of that knowledge with you – things that I've discovered about driving around the roads of Britain, rules that might help make your journeys more bearable.

I understand only too well that driving isn't the joy or pleasure it once was. Our roads are overcrowded, drivers are much more stressed, and the expense of driving has hit an all-time high. Add to this other, controversial, new factors such as speed cameras and congestion charging and it's not surprising that Britain's motorists are feeling fed up, put upon, and under attack. I reckon those of you who traverse our roads daily – commuters, mums on the school run, reps, taxi drivers, coach drivers, delivery drivers, and of course truckers – could all do with a little help. Don't despair. I've learned that some of these stresses can be circumvented, you don't always have to sit in miles of traffic, and a few simple ideas can make your life much easier.

In recent years, Radio 2 has become the most listened to station in the country, and I want to tell you something about the way we work, and in particular how the traffic news is created and presented, the times it's gone wrong, the times when my heart races, and my special relationship with the truckers of Great Britain.

Above all, I want to show you the fun side of driving and how you can get the most out of your mileage. It's not all doom and gloom, and driving can still be a pleasure if you plan it properly. Some of the most beautiful and scenic routes in the world are right here on our doorstep, from the lochs of Scotland to the coastal routes of Cornwall.

So, despite the queues, the delays, the speed cameras, the congestion charges, and the Green Guilt, the drivers of Great Britain seem to take everything in their stride and, well, just get on with it. You're all heroes to me, and this book is dedicated to you all.

Oh, and by the way, my traffic hotline number is 08700 100 200. I'll be waiting for your call!

INTRODUCTION

Poor old Dad (and me!)

Chapter One

The Long and Winding Road to Radio 2

*'Roads are literally the pathways, not only of
industry, but of social and national intercourse.'*
Sir Thomas Telford

R oads and cars seem to have been a constant throughout
my life. It appears that I have unwittingly continued a
family tradition that started almost two generations ago
with my grandfather working at the Austin motor works in
Longbridge, Birmingham.

Longbridge was one of Britain's longest running and most
renowned car factories, founded by Herbert Austin, later Sir
Herbert, in 1905. Austin was born in the Chilterns in 1866,
and after a brief stint in Australia he came back to England
to work for a car company set up by his friend Frederick
Wolseley. He left after ten years to found his own.

The site at Longbridge was discovered when Herbert
Austin's youngest daughter, Zeta Lambert, suggested that
her dad and the entire staff of three at the Austin Motor
Company should explore the area around Birmingham for a
new site. So they set off, in his Wolseley 7.5hp, complete
with a picnic basket attached to the front, and discovered a

disused printworks at Longbridge. Austin just knew it was right, and his staff moved in later that week. The first car manufactured there was a conventional 5-litre, four-cylinder model with chain drive; about 200 were made in the first five years.

My granddad worked at the plant all his life, almost from the inception of the company, as a Master Carpenter. Aside from having a real talent for carpentry, he was devoted to all things mechanical. There is a story handed down through the family that he was the first man in Birmingham to own a motorbike and sidecar, and I have a distant, but clear, memory of once sitting in that sidecar on a day out in Rhyl. He could almost touch the factory from his house, so near did he live to it, and I remember him leaving to walk to work each day with a box of sandwiches made and packed by Nanny Bo, his wife. The plant at Longbridge is now closed, but my affection for the Austin cars of that era lives on. Family folklore says that if you see any Austin motor car built before the Second World War, it's likely that our granddad created the woodwork. Imagine those elegant walnut dashboards! The wooden steering wheels! Working at the plant instilled in him a lifelong love of cars, which he passed onto his son, my dad.

My dad had run away from home to join the Army when he was only 17 years old; I suppose it was his little rebellion because his mother had told him he couldn't. He met my mum when he was posted to Windsor in Berkshire, and she was home on leave from the WAAF (Women's Auxiliary Air Force), visiting her family. Even she had a connection with transport, because she was a 'plotter' based near Christchurch, helping to guide RAF planes back to base on their return, usually from Germany. Just after they got married they had their first child, Bill. Dad was then posted overseas and only came back occasionally. He must have come home pretty regularly at Christmas times, though, because both my brother Peter and I are September babies. His army career eventually led him back home permanently, when he joined the RASC (the Royal Army Service Corps) and then the REME (the Royal Electrical and Mechanical Engineers). Both these regiments were involved with vehicles and engineering, which were areas of interest that fascinated dad throughout his life.

He had owned a succession of cars throughout my childhood. They were old, cheap, and usually black, but always beautiful. He would spend hours with his head under the bonnet, his body under the car, and his heart racing with excitement. He had always been a member of the Automobile Association, in the days when members of the AA proudly adorned the front of their cars with a beautiful chrome and yellow badge, and a smart AA patrolman would

Did you know?

The very first motorway was the Preston Bypass in Lancashire, which is today part of the M6 and M55. Originally it was eight miles in length, and had two lanes each way with a wide central reservation for the provision of a future third lane.

always salute you as he passed. There is an urban myth that says if the patrolman did not salute you, it meant there was a speed trap ahead. An increase in traffic meant they stopped saluting completely in 1965, so, speed traps or not, this charming custom was relegated to history. My own memory of these men on bikes is that they always seemed proud of their jobs; they sat up straight, usually with a side-car, and when you saw one you instantly felt safe. So what if you broke down, burst a tyre, or ran out of petrol? This Superman of the road would rescue you.

Did you know?

The busiest motorway section in Britain is widely reported to be the M25 between the A30 and the Heathrow Spur (Junctions 13 to 14). However, in 2005 a close contender was the M60 north of Manchester, between Junctions 16 and 17.

In those days, motorists were not the beleaguered group they have now become. It was a joy to drive on largely uncongested roads, without the Green Guilt and the tax. Drivers like my dad felt they were true pioneers, and experienced a thrill of heady excitement every time they ventured out. As children we shared this excitement, and travelling even short distances was genuinely exhilarating.

I remember one of dad's cars in particular. He had always wanted a Rolls-Royce, but because we couldn't afford one he bought the poor man's version: an Armstrong Siddeley. It was in terrible condition, but became his obsession.

Siddeleys were first made in 1919, but don't exist any more – neither does the famous Sphinx that adorned many a bonnet. They were a truly British car made by a British manufacturer, and were held in high regard by car lovers everywhere. Dad tinkered with his endlessly, but it never really worked properly. Maybe that was the point.

We once drove around Hyde Park Corner in it, just him and me, and it broke down in the middle lane of the one-way system, just before turning into Park Lane. I remember feeling utterly embarrassed as it spluttered and smoked to a halt. As he pushed it to the side of the road (muttering that he'd once again bought a 'pig in a poke' – I remember the phrase exactly), piles of traffic hooted for us to get out of the way.

Other cars came and went over the years, but nothing ever replaced the Armstrong Siddeley in his heart. It was the nearest thing to a Rolls that he ever owned.

Dad loved to take the family on drives, and most summer weekends he and my mum would pack my brothers and I into whatever car he had at the time, and just drive. Somewhere. Anywhere. He used to tell us we were going on a 'mystery trip', which usually meant another trudge down the A3 to Southsea. We tried to be surprised when we got there, but sometimes it was a struggle. When we did finally get there we always had a picnic, sometimes sitting in the car park, or sometimes on the beach. What I clearly remember are the empty peanut butter jars my mother filled with orange squash, which we'd drink with a straw pushed through a hole she'd made in the lid.

He took us on the M1 not long after it had been built, and

I remember the look of excitement in his eyes as he looked into the distance at nothing but concrete. I also remember driving along in pouring rain when the wipers on his old Ford Prefect stopped working. But we found a bit of string, connected it to the wipers, and then threaded it through the little quarter-light window in the front-seat passenger's door. Then I sat there pulling the string to make the wipers work, so that the windscreen was clear for him to see through.

He was a wonderful bloke, and still the funniest man I ever knew. To have lost him when he was only 57 years old was a tragedy, and I still miss him. Mum survived for another 12 years after his death, but life was never the same for her, and she was reunited with him in 2001.

So, through my dad – and, I suppose, his dad – I've been involved in driving and cars almost since I was born, and definitely since I can remember. I took my test the moment I could at the age of 17, and passed first time. In a strange twist of fate, I was driving around Hyde Park Corner in my first car, a Hillman Imp, not long afterwards and ran into the back of another car, bringing the whole of the one-way system to a halt. My dad would have been proud.

Soon I was driving everywhere. I named my first car Esmeralda, and she became my best friend. I once drove her to Cornwall from London in seven hours, and then had to leave her in a compound while I sailed to the Isles of Scilly. I felt like a mum abandoning her child for the first time, and fretted until we were safely reunited. One day, she died. I had to send her to the knacker's yard for five pounds. I clearly remember the morning of her removal. It was the middle of winter, and she was parked just round the corner from my little bed-sit. I sat inside her, wrapped up in a scarf, and cried, trying to explain why we were having to part. I still get upset when I have to get rid of my cars, but,

Did you know?

The pre-motorway era A580 (the East Lancs Road) running between Liverpool and Manchester was the first purpose-built inter-city highway to be constructed.

like a first love, it's never been as bad as losing Esmeralda.

Learner

I had always wanted to be an actress, so I was packed off to stage school at an early age. This meant that when I left school, I wasn't really qualified for anything much other than standing on a stage reciting lines. The problem was that I really wasn't that good at it, but nonetheless I trudged the length and breadth of the country performing in schools, halls and theatres. I once did a season with Butlins Holiday Camp's Repertory Company in Pwhelli, North Wales. We performed a different play from the repertory every night, and although you could bring children along, parents could, if they wanted, leave children in their chalets and a listening device could pick up any crying. This information was then relayed to the parents sitting in the theatre on a large screen at the side of the stage. Thus you could be halfway through a scene, giving it your all, when an announcement would come across the tannoy for Mr and Mrs Smith to please go and attend to their child, currently crying in chalet number 87, whilst at the same time this information flashed up on the screen next to you. I suppose it seemed a good idea at the time, but from a performer's point of view it was all a bit disheartening. All eyes turned to the screen at various times throughout the play, making us feel like bit players in a babysitting competition. I also remember that one night there was a heavy storm raging outside, and the entire company's words were drowned out as the rain fell on the tin roof above us. It was like watching a silent movie.

I couldn't face any more, so I decided to try other things. I worked for a while in a publishing company (the literary end of show business), then packed myself off, belatedly, to college, where I studied drama teaching. I really wasn't teaching material either. On one of my teaching practices I got hauled into the principal's office and asked why I locked a particularly troublesome 14-year-old in a stationery cupboard for ten minutes. His mother had, rightly, complained and I was on the verge of being thrown off the course. I wasn't, but realised that rude and spotty 14-year-olds weren't really my idea of a glittering career.

After college I had a job for a few years at the old London Weekend Television company, in their current affairs department, where I worked alongside a young researcher called Greg Dyke. When he got promoted, I was recommended to be a researcher for a particular project he was in charge of. He wouldn't let me do it because he didn't think I could hack it. When he finally became Director General of the BBC some years later, we bumped into each other in a lift, and I had to gloat. 'You thought I was rubbish all those years ago,' I said. 'Look at me now, doing traffic news!' His look of knowing said it all. Yes, Sally, that's really, well, great.

I got my first 'roads' job at the Automobile Association. At the time I applied for the job, I had no idea of the direction I was headed; I'd tried so many things, but nothing seemed to be exciting, or worthwhile. I'd even started to sing in a band. Singing had always been a great love, and by now I knew a great many musicians, mainly through going to gigs in clubs and pubs, but also through my brother, Bill, who was, and is, one of the greatest blues guitarists in the country.

My father was a wonderful pianist, always in demand at parties, and my son, Harry, has inherited this musical gene and is on the verge of a great musical career himself. I saw myself as a great pop star, a musical star, a diva even, and eventually joined a band, first as a backing singer and then as the one up front. We trawled the pubs of South London, mainly Clapham I seem to remember. Years later, I sang with a great pianist called Matthew Platt, writing songs and performing in clubs and at weddings and festivals, that sort of thing. Only recently have I stopped performing regularly, but hardly anything gives me greater pleasure than standing in a dingy club, with a piano, singing from my soul. As a long-term career, though, it was never meant to be. Seems that the universe wanted me as a traffic reporter, not as the next Barbra Streisand.

I really wanted to try presenting, and had been on a course, where I did reasonably well. The tutor said I should pursue it, so I did. The AA had set up Roadwatch in 1973, just as commercial radio in the UK was taking off. They felt there was a need to collate fast and accurate road traffic information, which at the time didn't really exist but was seen as being important to the development of motoring in general. I saw an advertisement asking for presenters and applied. I duly got an interview, and they seemed impressed by my TV background, but I heard nothing for ages.

Then, one day, I went home from work in the middle of the afternoon because I didn't feel well. This was something I hardly ever did, and I remember the day very clearly. I walked in to my little flat, hadn't even taken my raincoat off, and the phone rang. I didn't have an answerphone then, and mobile phones didn't exist, so had I not walked in at that precise moment I would never have got the call, or had the subsequent conversation. It was the AA. They had found a candidate for the job, but it turned out he didn't want it after all and I was next on their list. Of course, I accepted the job. But I often wonder what would have happened in the years following had I not walked into my flat at that very moment. It seems that an angel had stepped into my life and showed me a direction: I was to be a traffic reporter! This sort of thing

Hah Hah Hah!

The Policeman couldn't believe his eyes as he saw the woman drive past him, busily knitting. Quickly he drew alongside the vehicle, wound down his window and shouted: 'Pull over!' 'No,' she replied, 'they're socks!'

has happened often, when I've been at my most confused or uncertain in which direction I should go. Something comes along and steers me. Such things are part of the mystery of life that continues to fascinate and excite me.

I joined Roadwatch in the early 1980s when it was still in its infancy, and six of us sat in a tiny office at the back of an enormous hangar of a room in which rows of people at desks took breakdown calls, watched over by a supervisor from a little raised platform. This individual kept a weather eye on us, too, so it was a bit like being back at school. If the phone operators even wanted to go to the toilet they had to put their hands up to ask permission, so that the supervisor knew where they were at all times.

Back then, proper traffic information was hard to come by. The unit had been set up with the idea that AA patrols would radio in with any problems on the roads that they had personally experienced. However, although that sometimes happened we were mostly at the mercy of police forces, who would tell us the state of the roads in their area, but even that information was often late and out of date. So driving back then could be a lonely old business, and anyone who spent time driving around the country got very little help. Remember, this was in the days before police cameras, mobile phones and the internet.

Even so, although our traffic news might not have been terribly useful I think we started a bit of a trend, and soon traffic reports started popping up everywhere. Even if they were out of date they definitely generated a feeling that if you weren't in a jam you'd heard about, then you were OK.

But mainly the job served as great training. As broadcasters, we hopped from one station to the next in a matter of seconds, often delivering information to as many as 12 stations an hour. I admit to getting confused once in a while, and telling the folks of Oxfordshire what was happening in London, or vice versa, but I learned and learned. So from early on I became familiar with the M1, the M40, the M25 and other major roads across the south-east of the country. Actually, when I began the M25 hadn't even been completed, there was no bus lane on the M4 coming into London from Heathrow, and the M6 Toll Road was a distant dream. So in a way, parts of the modern motorway system and I have grown up together.

By then I'd driven a lot, and understood how important it was for drivers to get the proper information. It gave me enormous pleasure to get thank-yous and plaudits when I did get it right, but I was also very aware that a lot of our information was probably wrong. Despite this, I discovered that I loved being 'on air' – it felt very natural and I seldom got nervous. I started to feel that I'd finally stumbled onto something worthwhile.

Passing my test

So I'd begun to learn my trade, I suppose. Not that it was all smooth going. I was once late for a broadcast and ran into the studio from about 50 yards away, and of course the whole thing sounded awful as I tried to catch my breath. Lesson learned. Then there was the time I accidentally left a fader open on the broadcasting desk and slagged off someone at the station I was about to broadcast to. Another lesson learned. But it was an exciting time for me because I really felt that I'd found a niche for myself; everything that I had done up until then seemed to be

coming together, and I knew the direction I wanted to take. Not only was I enjoying the job, but I'd finally found something I was good at.

After several happy years at Roadwatch, I left to get married and have Harry, my son; my husband had accepted a job overseas, so I spent Harry's first five years really just being a mum, which is something I shall never regret. Harry has turned out to be the light of my life, the proudest thing I have ever, or will ever, achieve. From the moment he was born until now, he has hardly ever let me or his dad down, and continues to bring joy into our lives each day. Life has not always been easy for him, with a full-time working mum and parents who separated when he was very young, but somehow he's turned out perfectly.

It was because of that separation, when Harry was about five years old, that I needed a job again. Fortunately, at exactly this moment Roadwatch invited me back to broadcast some of the first bulletins on Classic FM, which had just been born and was the first station to deliver national traffic bulletins. This proved to be great experience for the future, but at the time I felt hampered and disappointed by the lack of real-time information. Mobile phones were then just coming into use, so some information was much more immediate, but I still felt that I was short-changing drivers.

At around this time I started doing occasional traffic news shifts at GLR (Greater London Radio), the local BBC station for London. Their traffic bulletins came from studios at Scotland Yard, and I couldn't believe how different it was, because suddenly I had access to *police cameras*! This tiny studio gave me free rein to see, at first hand, all the jams across London. I became so adept at using these cameras that I would broadcast and flip between them at the same time, so I really was able to get a true picture. In fact the 'click-click' of the cameras changing at the same time that I spoke annoyed one of the Governors of the station so much that I was asked to stop doing it. I did for a bit, but it wasn't half as efficient. This was the first time I realised that lofty souls on the periphery of broadcasting have no clue about what the listeners actually want to hear, so I resumed my

Did you know?

How are A and B roads numbered? The numbering is based on nine zones which cover the mainland of Britain, numbered 1 to 9: all the roads that start in a given zone take the first digit of their route number from the zone number (so roads in the 5 zone include the A511 and B5203, for instance). The zones are defined by the roads A1 to A9 and the coast.

clicking and fortunately it was never mentioned again. I finally felt like I was giving the poor old driver value for money. The station eventually offered me a full-time job, so I left Roadwatch and began a new phase of my career.

My time at GLR coincided with that of a chap who occasionally presented shows that I would contribute to: Johnnie Walker. I had no idea then that this intermittent pairing would ultimately result in changing my life utterly, but it was clear that this talented and legendary broadcaster had a knack of getting the best out of his on-air colleagues. I always looked forward to his slots because I knew we would have fun. Once we ended up singing the Beatles' *Yellow Submarine* together, although I can't remember why. We never actually saw each other then, because he was at the station based in Marylebone High Street, and I was at the Yard, as it were.

GLR was a great station overall, and has produced some of this country's finest broadcasters. Chris Evans got a big break there, and it's also where Vanessa Feltz got her start. Gideon Coe and Fi Glover presented one of the best breakfast shows I've ever heard, and have both gone on to prove themselves all-round brilliant broadcasters. It was during one of their breakfast shows that I presented a bulletin with a terrible cold. At the end of the bulletin I thought they'd faded me down, but they hadn't, and you heard me blowing my nose for Britain, in one long, painful blast.

In those pre-congestion-charge days the roads in and around London were usually pretty busy, but I felt that the traffic news we gave out was accurate because of the cameras. In fact, I learned through BBC research that it was one of the main reasons listeners tuned in to the station. This was a great boost for my self-confidence, and backed up my theory that if you got the information right, then people would trust the station as a whole. I now really believed that I understood how to do traffic news properly – and, more importantly, I knew I could never do it on my own: I needed 'eyes'.

Knowing the road

From the time I began working at GLR in 1992, and for the next 12 years both there and at Radio 2, I commuted daily between Surrey and London – I reckon I averaged around 30,000 miles a year, sometimes more. I'm aware that for some drivers this is neither very long nor very far, and that many commuters and professional drivers spend years trudging the same route daily, locked in a vehicle, usually dreading what may lie ahead. But those 12 years taught me about the grim reality of the daily commute, and the frustration it can cause. The whole journey is spent worrying about what awful delay might befall you, what accidents may lie ahead, what roadworks there might be, and what happens if some idiot forgets to put his brakes on and runs clear into the back of you, or worse.

It was also during this time that I discovered how valuable proper traffic information could be. There's nothing worse than hopping in your car on a Friday evening, looking forward to a relaxing evening at home after what may have been a pretty terrible day (or week) at work, and then

NA 6840

Dad with the only car he ever really hated!

Dad with brothers Bill and Peter. Love the flat cap

Me aged two.
Butter wouldn't melt...

Dad, Mum,
brother Bill and
a friend. The car
is a Morris Minor
convertible – is Dad
trying to make it laugh?

Me trying to look cool
unaware there's a hole
in my dress...

Me and Paul
McCartney on the
Johnnie Walker show.

On stage in my singing days.
The people you can see were the
entire audience.

Harry aged 5, hamming it up for the camera. Don't know where he gets that from.

Traffic starts to build up on the M1 as soon as it is opened (Getty)

Spaghetti Junction: a mass of road knitting (Getty)

Motorists on the Severn Bridge just after it was opened (Getty)

At work trying to look as if I know what I'm doing...

Snuggling up to the Vine... (Day Macaskill)

immediately running into miles and miles of traffic. I have spent entire Friday nights on motorways, and cried in front of my steering wheel in frustration and anger. You suddenly realise that you won't have time to say goodnight to your kids, or you're going to miss the school play, or won't arrive in time for an appointment. I have experienced all these things, and know that a little help somewhere along the way could have transformed my timetable.

The truth is, though, that traffic news is often hard to get right. Anyone who says otherwise is lying! Things happen and change incredibly quickly. One minute you have a clear run ahead, and the next, the motorway has been closed because of a dreadful accident. The time it takes to get that information through to someone like me can make all the difference as to whether you get to see your child's school play or not. My own, wonderful, callers help enormously in this regard, and let me know immediately something happens in front of them. Though the detail is often difficult to grasp, and provides just a sketchy outline of the problem, I still try to get it across as quickly as I can so that avoiding action can be taken.

If and when I get it wrong there's usually someone ready to shout and scream at me down the phone, venting their frustration on the most accessible individual to hand. In the beginning I used to shout back, crushed that I had somehow not delivered, but now I'm calmer. I completely understand how they feel, and if I hear a stressed-out driver on the end of my phone I try to pick it up and give them some consolation. I never mind being shouted at now. If you want to yell at someone, please be my guest. I totally understand.

James Taylor making me swoon

Chapter Two

Life at Radio 2

*'When buying a used car, punch the buttons on
the radio. If all the stations are rock and roll,
there's a good chance the transmission is shot.'*
Larry Lucask, American DJ

I joined Radio 2 in 1998, as their first dedicated Traffic and
Travel reporter. Johnnie Walker had been offered the
Drivetime slot after the legendary John Dunn's departure.
John, who had hosted the show for many years, had developed
the most incredible relationship with listeners across the UK
and Johnnie's arrival raised a few eyebrows. They needn't have
worried. Within a very short space of time listeners took him to
their hearts, and his mixture of fun, serious topics and, above
all, great music won everyone over. He also realised that traffic
news at that time of day was vital, which is where I came in.

I had grown fond of GLR, but it had changed. Even
though the ratings were fantastic, the BBC had decided that
more speech, less music, was required. This prompted an
enormous backlash amongst listeners, who campaigned
vigorously to keep the station as it had been, but in the end
they lost. This left me in a difficult position: presenters left,

there was much less music, and, five years on, I was myself ready to move. My angel came along again at just the right time. I clearly remember going into work one morning and standing at the window, looking out, and wondering what to do next. I did my shift, and went home. In exactly the same way as it had happened before, I walked into the house and the phone rang. I still had my coat on.

'Hello, Boazman, it's Johnnie Walker here. How do you fancy singing *Yellow Submarine* on Radio 2 with me?' It was the start of what we now call a 'special relationship'. They had auditions for other people, but I won the day. At first GLR refused to let me go, as I still had some time left to run on my contract with them. But I knew I couldn't let the moment pass, so gave them notice and just left. I just knew it was right.

I don't know how, or why, but Johnnie and I seemed to bond with the listeners right from the start. These things can't be planned, or passed through a focus group. They either work or they don't. He was always incredibly generous to me on air, and after a shy start, and with his help and encouragement, I got into my stride. The banter was great, but I never forgot the real reason I was there, which was to try and cover as much traffic news as possible in the time allotted to me, and that's still the case with whichever presenter I'm working alongside.

Up until the time I began at Radio 2, the traffic news was simply read out by the main presenter on the show. It was something that had been prepared for them beforehand, and it was usually out of date and therefore largely irrelevant. So when I came along, I knew that unless we could give out

Did you know?

Who puts up road signs? Whoever maintains the road – either a national organisation or a local authority. The AA and RAC, the two principal motoring clubs, were permitted to erect their own permanent road signs, to government standards, until the early 1960s. Today they still have permission to erect temporary event signposting, which can often be seen around the country. These are yellow for the AA and blue for the RAC.

reliable information we'd fail. I understood that the credibility of a massive station like Radio 2 was on the line, and that if I got it wrong all the time the whole station would look daft.

I'd become used to getting real information from Scotland Yard's police cameras, so desperately needed new 'eyes'. I wanted to talk about jams that were happening in real-time, so I set up a phone line to see if I could get more accurate information. Once listeners realised that they could telephone in, and help *everyone* out, the phone started ringing off the hook.

I was incredibly well supported at the time by Radio 2's management team; they really seemed to understand what I was trying to do, and, more importantly, came to see that what I was doing seemed to be working. Jim Moir, then Radio 2 controller, simply left me to develop the idea myself, and never really interfered. He seemed to understand how important it was to get it right, which helped a lot. Lesley Douglas, then his deputy and now his successor, has always been equally supportive, so I have been exceptionally lucky. Not all radio bosses have the same insight or are as encouraging. But I did get carried away a bit at first, and early on I had a visit from a member of management who asked me not to ramble so much. He was probably right, but at the time I was so thrilled to be able to give out so much information, and was so encouraged by the listeners' reactions, that I knew instinctively something new and groundbreaking was happening.

This was borne out in the first couple of years, when rival stations started imitating the style and content of the Radio 2 traffic news. One even put a female traffic reporter in place and named her Sally Beauman, and tried to get her to interact with her presenter in the same way I did with Johnnie Walker. This wasn't her real name, of course, but so successful had the Radio 2 traffic news become that everyone wanted to copy it.

From the very beginning, what I did seemed to resonate with the driving public, in particular with truckers and other professional drivers who have a lonely old job at the best of times. Suddenly, they knew they had an ally, someone who really did care

Did you know?

Who designs the road signs? There are set designs for each sign, which were initially established in the 1960s by the Worboys Committee. The typeface and many of the symbols and pictograms were designed by noted graphic artists Jock Kinneir and Margaret Calvert.

if they got stuck in a jam, or couldn't get their delivery in on time. What a presenter can't do is *pretend* to care. Fake or feigned interest always comes across as exactly that, as does a lack of understanding of what you're talking about. But I think the drivers know now, and knew then, that I understand and care about them, and that I'm a friend who wants to help them out.

Nor do I just want to help professional drivers. I want to help every driver who, for whatever reason, needs decent, accurate information. I once had a call from a lady who was stuck in driving rain, which was coming down so hard I could hear it in the background. She was almost in tears, scared to drive on, and wondering what she should do. I couldn't get to the call, but reassured her soon after on the air that if she took it easy, or even pulled over until the storm had passed, she'd be fine. That incident taught me that the relationship between listener and traffic reporter can be very, very special, investing trust and affection on both sides. I hope she got home OK.

Since new regulations came in regarding hand-held phones in cars, reporting jams is different – that lady could not phone now without fear of prosecution unless she had already pulled over. This applies to all drivers, of course, and I never, *ever*, encourage them to ring in unless they're on hands-free sets, which are now used by professional and non-professional drivers alike. Although the quality is sometimes like having a conversation with someone at the bottom of a toilet, at least the information manages to get through.

Some callers have been with me from the beginning, others have joined along the way, but they mostly remain devoted Radio 2 listeners. If it wasn't for them I wouldn't be able to do the job, so they know I love them. I have enormous respect for anyone who drives for a living, whether they're truckers, coach drivers, taxi drivers, van drivers, or couriers. They make all of our lives so much easier, and are always under-appreciated. The fact is, without them we would have very little. Even the houses we live in are built from bricks delivered by road. Then there's the food, the electrical goods, the furniture...the list goes on and on. So the next time you see one of these professional vehicles, give them a break and say a little thank-you. Some people say they clog up our roads too much, but until the politicians come up with a better way to deliver goods let's be kind. They're not always perfect, but without them you probably wouldn't be driving in your car in the first place.

With friends like these...

I spend my days talking and listening to drivers, working as hard as I can for them, and our affection is deep-seated. Most drivers have 'handles' (names that they've conjured up for themselves) which generally describe an aspect of their personality. This is a leftover from the days of CB radio, when drivers were recognised by their callsigns as they spoke to each other across the country. Back then it was the drivers themselves who transmitted information about road problems between each other, and that still happens to some extent today. (CB radios seem to have escaped the legislation that applies to mobile phones, so are still a means of communication for large numbers of professional drivers.)

The names they come up with can be incredibly witty, from Lord of the Pies to Geordie Armani; from Perry Comb-Over, to Nice But Dim. And they make me smile, sometimes even giggle: who else can boast calls from Major Overdraft, Eileen Dover and Badly Overdrawn Boy in one morning? Some of them cheekily try to give something commercial a plug. Range Rover Ron is one that springs to mind. Then there was Carlsberg Carl and HP Sauce Man. Nice try chaps, but I'm not allowed to – really!

I was once asked by a presenter what my own 'handle' could be. I didn't know, but an enterprising listener rang in to suggest Golden Eagle, and it turned out to be my favourite. Why? Because, in his words, 'She's a big bird, but bloody lovely to look at.'

On days like these...

A typical day at work involves fielding hundreds of calls, checking and double-checking information as it comes in, and getting it on the air as quickly as possible. I've said it many times, but without the help of the drivers out there on the road my job would be impossible. And I'm lucky, because Radio 2 has so many millions of listeners. My 'pool' is much larger than my competitors', so I can always guarantee that if anything major happens on either a motorway or a major A road then I'll hear about it first. The generosity of my listeners is always astounding, and always very welcome.

Of course, sometimes motorists get frustrated when they get stuck in a jam, and if I've got it wrong, or haven't mentioned their particular queue, they phone up and have a rant. One caller got so upset that he threatened to iron my shirt with his motor, which made me tremble slightly, but he later called back to apologise. I once even got a murder threat, simply because I hadn't mentioned a delay affecting this poor person. The BBC took it seriously at the time, but I'm still here. Who'd have thought a traffic reporter's life could be so, well, *racy*? Expectations about how I can help are, self-evidently, very high, and it's a lot to live up to.

But I always understand. As I've said, I've been in tears when stuck in jams from which I can't escape and am suddenly late for something really important. Your palms sweat, your heart races, and nothing you can do will make any difference. Traffic jams cost the British economy £5 billion a year, so it's important that I try to get it right as often as possible.

And if you do ever call in to tell me about a problem, please don't say 'Hello Sally *and team*...' What team would that be,

Did you know?

The widest motorway section is the M61 at Linnyshaw Moss, Greater Manchester (close to the M60 interchange), which has 17 separate traffic lanes side by side, spread across several parallel carriageways. In fact, a look on the ground makes it clear that there are actually 18 parallel lanes for a very short stretch (aerial photographs confirm this).

then? It's just me, a phone, and a computer, so no wonder it's not always perfect! With a two-minute bulletin, it's sometimes hard to pack everything in. But I promise I try.

The daily grind

12:00–12:30pm: Arrive at work. Get coffee and nick leftover goodies from Wogan's, Bruce's and Kennedy's studios. Sausages are often involved. Although we hardly ever see each other, I understand they're the best-fed presenters at the station!

12:40pm: Say 'Hi' to the Jeremy Vine team; check what Jeremy's wearing, to see if I can tease him later…I usually can. Jeremy is wonderful, and a great giggler. For such a serious programme, we spend a lot of time laughing. Of course, he always takes his subjects seriously, but he once had to read out a list of the ten most embarrassing things to see your doctor about. This was to encourage people to phone in and talk about these things openly and unashamedly. But after the first one, which I think was genital warts, I was on the floor. By the time he got to ulcers in your bottom, he was too.

1:00pm: Prepare my first bulletin whilst watching Steve Wright's guests arrive out of the corner of my eye. They are always incredibly famous, sometimes with massive entourages in tow. There was once a diva so famous that she had 12 minders, all big and muscular and miserable. Why do minders always look so miserable? Anyway, one of them stood outside the studio door and wouldn't let me in to do my traffic bulletin. I threw a few choice words in his direction and seconds later I was sitting in my usual place. I never cease to wonder why these famous celebrities have so many people around them. I don't know how they'd survive if they had to actually hail a taxi on their own, or, worse, drive their own vehicle. Of course, there are equally famous people who simply arrive on their own, sit quietly until it's their turn, and are utterly charming. Strange how those with all the people in tow are often exactly the opposite.

This is the time I check the telephone messages, look up incidents, and check the queues. If something big is happening, or happens during this period, I quickly write a script and hand it to Jeremy, so that drivers are warned before my first bulletin. But if Jeremy is in the middle of an interview with the Prime Minister or some other intellectual giant then you might have to wait.

1:25pm: Read the first bulletin of the day with Jeremy Vine. By now I have a clear picture of the jams across the country, and begin to get into my stride. This can be a quiet time, which is just as well as I often end up reading my bulletin sitting between, say, the Home Secretary and the US Ambassador. But if it's just Jeremy and I, then after the traffic news we can chat or comment about the stories he's doing, make a joke (usually at my expense) or just move on if he's waiting to read out serious listener comments. Jeremy is another presenter who took a lot of flak when he replaced

Jimmy Young, and proved to me again how much listeners hate change. I was also the subject of a lot of criticism when I first arrived – who the hell was this woman who kept cropping up every half an hour? But Jeremy has proved himself a popular presenter and an essential part of the Radio 2 line-up; his interviewing technique is such that no one is ever allowed to get away with spin or evasion. He always knows his stuff, and is highly regarded by listeners and interviewees alike. But a sense of fun, underlying his seriousness, also comes through, endearing him to me and to the nation.

2:45pm: Time for my first bulletin with the amazing Steve Wright. Steve has always been wonderful to me. His broadcasting skills are legendary, and his programme pulls in millions of listeners. He and his team work incredibly hard to produce three hours of brilliant radio every day, which is always guaranteed to entertain and inform. Steve himself has always understood the importance and relevance of what I do, and allows me to interrupt his programme whenever I have something to say. As a driver himself, he really does understand. He has a unique perspective on everything to do with radio because of his long association with the medium. There's nothing he doesn't know about broadcasting, or what it is that listeners want. He also has a reputation as a fair and entertaining interviewer, which is why every celebrity in the world wants to be on his show. Through Steve I've sat next to everyone I've ever heard of, people such as Charlton Heston, Whitney Houston, Mickey Rooney, George Michael, Gene

Wilder...and they all fight to come on, because of him and his reputation.

From here on I'm on air every half hour, slotting in between guests, factoids, and the team. I get very scared when there's a hugely famous person sitting next to me. When Paul McCartney came in I couldn't face him and do the bulletin at the same time, so I apologised and turned my back towards him. He spent the whole two minutes running his finger up and down my back! It's amazing I got through it at all.

I have always been a huge fan of James Taylor, and when he came in for an interview on the Johnnie Walker Drivetime Show some years ago I simply couldn't stop shaking. The thought of sitting next to one of my absolute heroes, who, by the way, I also fancied, was almost too much, and I warned Johnnie that my bulletin might well be a mess. It was. But one of the most sublime moments of my life was sitting a foot away from him while he sang *The Secret o' Life*, one of my favourite songs. I was in tears by the end of it. I fell completely in love with this wonderful, funny, man. Before he left the studio he kissed and hugged me, which nearly made me faint. I've met him several times now, been to every concert he's done in the UK for the past eight years, and always get a hug, a kiss and a chat backstage afterwards. He's one of the nicest men in the world, and pictures of us together adorn my home and are the wallpaper on my computer. If it sounds like I'm a bit obsessed, then that's probably because I am.

The worst thing is those heroes who turn out to be, well,

less than you expected. There's one famous actor who I'd always had a thing for. I'd seen all his films, thought his acting was superb, and adored him from afar. Imagine my thrill then when I knew he was coming in for an interview. I did the make-up extra carefully, put on a great, short, dress, and waited. He sat outside my office, with two press representatives, and I waited for a good opportunity to go and shake his hand. But while they were waiting I couldn't help but overhear the conversation, and he was a right idiot. He was affected, pompous, and had no sense of humour. I didn't ever go and say hello. My hero was a total numptie.

I will never get used to meeting all these famous people, though – like Peter Noone of Herman's Hermits popping in to my office to use my computer; Bob Geldof looking at the map on my wall; Steve Harley

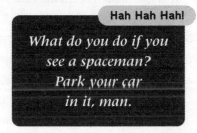

always popping in for a chat whenever he's in the building; Rod Stewart gripping my knee while I was trying to do a bulletin sitting next to him; and Roger Daltry always saying 'Hi' when he's around.

Status Quo once made me a birthday card at the last minute when they were in for an interview and realised it was my big day. Not long after, for one of their tours, they asked me to make recordings to kick off their shows; so at the start of each show, in each different town, you could hear my voice resounding around the venue telling people to avoid the area because of massive amounts of traffic heading towards them – all backed up by fantastic guitar riffs. What a thrill!

Paul McCartney always comes in for a hug whenever he's around; he was once there when my son Harry came in to see me. As Paul and I said 'Hi' and had a chat, I turned around to introduce Harry to him. But poor Harry was rooted to the spot and could hardly speak. One of the most famous men in the world was talking to his mum, and Harry just couldn't get over it!

Another lovely bloke is Robert Plant, who is always warm and charming. He sang at Bob Harris's 60th Birthday party, in a barn in Oxfordshire, where he was on stage with the amazingly talented guitarist Bernie Marsden, of Whitesnake fame. Another great band, the Storys, had played beforehand, and when it came time for Robert and Bernie to get on the little raised platform at the end of the barn they were without a drummer. I can't remember whose idea it was, but suddenly Brian Thomas, the drummer from the

Did you know?

The narrowest motorway section in the country is the A601(M), which is single-carriageway between the M6 roundabout and Over Kellet (where it ends on a B road). The A6144(M) was also a contender, being entirely single-carriageway, but was downgraded in May 2006 and is no longer a motorway. It was built to a substantially higher standard than the A601(M)'s southern section.

Storys, got behind them and played. He spent the whole set with a look of utter surprise and horror on his face – suddenly, unexpectedly, he was part of a supergroup! There are many famous rock stars who would not have done what Robert Plant did that night, so in my mind he'll always be a top bloke. And to be standing in a small room, with him singing just feet in front of you, is something I shall never forget. Bob Harris and his wife, Trudi, are themselves extremely special people. They're loved and respected by almost everyone I know, and the depth of that respect was reflected in the fact that one of the greatest rock singers of our time was prepared to turn up and sing at his friend's birthday party in a barn.

This association with old rockers meant I was asked to present acts at GuilFest one year. This annual music festival in Guildford puts on some of the greatest acts around, both past and present, and is a great festival for all the family. I spent the days there hanging around backstage with the likes of Rolf Harris, Steve Harley, the Levellers, Simple Minds and Katie Melua while they waited for their entrances. Between acts I went out to pump up the crowds before they went on. This was fine until I realised that no one actually wanted to either hear or see me, they just wanted the band – so I mostly ran on stage quickly, said the name, and ran off again.

These things are the joy of the job, and I am always in awe, and I am always a fan. Usually.

Once an incredibly famous American singer came in to the studios and complained that she'd had to sit next to a 'traffic reporter' in the middle of her interview. Another apparently told the producer that I'd smelt unpleasant. I didn't, but at least my face was intact. Not only was hers not intact, but she'd had so many peels you could see right through it.

But I have also discussed nail varnish with Mariah Carey, and perfume with Janet Jackson. Lovely.

5:15pm: Drivetime. It's now the busiest time of my day. The calls come in thick and fast, and as I move in to sit opposite Chris Evans I'm starting to flag. Fortunately Chris and his team have enough energy between them to light up the Post Office Tower, so I'm rejuvenated.

The Drivetime slot was a hard one to fill after Johnnie Walker left, and Chris Evans took a beating when it was announced that he was to take over. It was, again, a reflection of how listeners really don't like change, and of course, Johnnie had developed a close and fantastic relationship with them during his seven years on the show. I'd also felt unsettled at Johnnie's departure, and had another of those 'what-should-I-do-with-my-life?' moments. But this time no angel came along to tell me to move on, so I looked forward – with some trepidation, it has to be said – to working with another broadcasting legend. It was a big change for me, because I knew that I'd miss my old sparring partner terribly. But Chris really is fantastic. From the beginning he's been kind, thoughtful, and extremely generous on and off air. I've grown to love working with him and the rest of the team. Listeners ultimately decide what they like to hear, and each presenter has their own devoted fans. But I really think you should know that Mr Evans is charming and caring and has engendered a fantastic team spirit. He's won over the team, and the nation, in a spectacular way.

I feel especially close to the Drivetime programme because that's where I began on Radio 2. In fact, when I first started it was the only programme that featured me and my traffic news, and it wasn't until a few months later that I got extended to Ed Stewart's afternoon show (before Steve Wright's reign began) and then to Jeremy Vine. So my track record with Drivetime is a long and affectionate one. Of course, as it's my busiest time I can get stressed, but Chris always understands and gives me space. He makes me feel supported and loved. All any woman could ask, really.

7:00pm: Time to go home.

7:30pm: A large G&T, with my feet up on the sofa. I ponder on the day's events, and if I've left with a big queue still building somewhere, I think about the drivers who might still be stuck. Note to self: must get a life.

But it doesn't always go according to plan

In the land of live radio so much can, and usually does, go wrong...

Like the time I was halfway through a bulletin on the Ken Bruce Show, when, inexplicably, my chair collapsed beneath

Did you know?

A staggering 60 per cent of all British truck drivers listen to Radio 2!

me, landing me on the floor. Cue lots of fat jokes.

Like the time I flirted outrageously on air with Pat Cash, the tennis player, and moved on smoothly – so I thought – into my traffic bulletin. My first item involved the Scottish place name 'Fullwood', but instead of saying that I said 'Fullcock'.

I've called the 'Strand Underpass' in London the 'Strand Underpants'.

I once referred to the road through 'Cockermouth' as being 'a bit sticky'.

I once heard from a reliable source that a petrol station had closed all of its pumps after a fire. It hadn't. They telephoned after hearing one of my bulletins, furious, and said that it explained why they'd had no customers for two hours.

I once said that the Forth Road Bridge was closed, so anyone travelling across the Clyde should think again. Whoops.

After I'd finished one bulletin, I had a showbiz tantrum and told a presenter to '*** off'. What I didn't know was that he'd kept the fader open, and six million people heard. Fortunately I kept my job, but only just.

An accident happened in Fochabars, Scotland, and I dreaded announcing it, for obvious reasons. I forewarned the presenter and producer so that they wouldn't draw attention to it, but of course they did. I couldn't read it without choking and guffawing and it sounded terrible. At the start of each subsequent bulletin, Mark Radcliffe, the presenter, insisted on asking how things were in the 'Scottish place that you find so difficult to say'. Unfortunately, the accident didn't clear for several hours, so my agony was never ending.

I once announced a traffic problem reported by someone who'd called himself Fur-Burger. I didn't know what it meant then, but I do now.

I was once in the middle of a traffic report with Jeremy Vine when the late great Sheridan Morley walked into the studio. He'd got lost, and, unaware that I was on air, he started to ask me the way to a particular studio area. I told him I was in the middle of something, but in his confusion he didn't grasp that it was a live bulletin and carried on asking for directions. I got the giggles, and couldn't finish, and when he finally left I collapsed. He must have thought I was incredibly rude. I never did understand if he realised that his questions about studios were going out live on air. Jeremy, of course, was no help at all and just sat opposite me giggling...

A phone-in contestant once rambled on to the presenter about how she couldn't stand me. But that's show biz.

And on Johnnie Walker's very last show I ended up dancing with Neil Diamond.

So it's not all bad.

Embarrassing place names

I've said some of these on air, but fortunately not all. I'm urging every single driver to *please* never have an accident in any of these places. And I'd be very grateful if local councils never installed roadworks in them either.

Balls Cross

Bell End

Bonar Bridge

Brown Willy

The Cock of Arran

Cock Bridge

Cockermouth

Cocks

Dull

Dyke

Fanny Hill

Fanny Burn

Fochabars

Hole

Lickey End

Lickham Bottom

Lord Hereford's Knob

North Piddle

Old Sodbury

Penistone

Pratts Bottom

Sandy Balls

Shitlingthorpe

Thong

Three Cocks

Tosside

Twathats

Twatt

Weedon

Wetwang

I declare...

Chapter Three

A Potholed History of British Roads and Transport

*'Let us travel, and whenever we find no facility for
travelling from a city to a town, from a village to a
hamlet, we may pronounce the people to be barbarians.'*
Abbé Raynal

Since earliest times, it seems that the best way to get from A to B in Great Britain has been by a road of some sort. In very early times the only practical way to travel was on foot or horseback. Then, the poor walked and the rich rode. But the Romans saved us and built a network of straight roads linking the main towns. For centuries after the Romans left, these roads continued to exist, and their remains can be traced even today. The legacy left by these early road-makers is everywhere. For instance, place names ending with 'Le Street' mark the line of roads between Roman settlements. Horses eventually gave way to stagecoaches, which became the way to travel, although these were incredibly uncomfortable at first as they had bodies that rested on axles placed rigidly parallel with each other. This is why roads remained straight – cornering could be, and was, very dangerous! It could take four days to travel by stagecoach from London to Dover along the Old Roman Watling Street, even though, at the time, it was considered to be one of the best roads in the country.

Coach drivers were the forerunners of today's truckers; they were incredibly skilled at their work, and many developed the 'four in hand technique' urging the horses to run ever faster, which made journeys quicker but still very, very bumpy. The coaching era, which eventually spanned many years, was a thrilling time and brought glamour and colour to the roads of Great Britain. But with early transport along poor roads came serious danger. Highwaymen lurked everywhere, and it was usual to sew money into your clothes so that you'd have spare change if everything else got nicked.

By 1555 a law had been passed which elected two 'surveyors of Highways' in each parish across the country. These characters were supposed to keep the peace on the roads, and watch out for potential criminals. Roads at this time were considered 'verie noisome and tedious to travel in, and dangerous to all passengers and carriages'. Three centuries earlier, in 1285, another law had been passed decreeing that bushes and trees should be cut back 200 feet either side of the road 'to prevent robbers from lurking therein'.

Travelling across the country increasingly became part of people's lives, although in 1749 it could take two days to travel from Glasgow to Edinburgh. In 1763 a coach company was set up which travelled between Edinburgh and London. This journey could take anything from 10 to 15 days, setting off once a month. And because of the hazardous nature of the journey, passengers were advised to make their wills before setting out!

Road surfaces were treacherous. Old roads were so unstable that they could sink to between 8 and 10 feet deep in bad weather. It's said that riders' heads could be lower than the ground level on either side. The fact was, these roads just couldn't cope.

Did you know?

Fictional road numbers are assigned for use on television and in films. And any road number involved in a serious fictional accident is blacklisted for five years from actual real-world use.

As the industrial revolution approached, so the number of horse-drawn carts and coaches increased, and Britain's dirt tracks weren't up to it. This became the era of the 'Turnpike Trusts'.

Turnpike Trusts were made up of groups of people who came together to buy a stretch of road and maintain it. They paid for this by taking toll money from those using the road. You can still see the evidence of these toll roads, some of them with a tiny house right on the edge of the road – this was the home of the Turnpike Trust's toll collector. By 1830 Turnpike Trusts looked after 20,000 miles of road. With industry developing and the population growing, these became the backbone of the country, rather like the motorways of today.

The Trusts marked the decline of dirt tracks and started an

Blind Jack of Knaresborough, the blind road-maker

John Metcalf was born in Knaresborough in 1717. At the age of six he contracted smallpox and became blind, but this didn't stop him from leading a life full of adventure and colour. After learning to ride and play the violin in his youth, he also became a strong swimmer. There's a story that despite his blindness he once rescued a man who was drowning in the River Nidd: hearing the man's screams, he leapt into the river and dragged him out.

At over six feet tall 'Blind Jack', as he became known, cut a distinguished and dashing figure. His reputation with the ladies was well known, and after fathering an illegitimate child he set off travelling around the country to escape the consequences. At that time he made his living as a violinist, but he eventually married and settled in Harrogate.

He first flirted with roads when he started a taxi service, transporting people between York and Knaresborough in the first one-horse chair in existence. This contraption looked a bit like a horse pulling a plough, except that there was a seat at the end of two long poles, which rested on two wheels. He made this journey once a week in winter, and twice a week in the summer. He never saw his blindness as a handicap, but how he negotiated the roads is a marvel. Those journeys must have taught him how unstable road surfaces could be, and it started him thinking. He ended up carrying fish from coastal towns to Leeds and Manchester, where he thought he could sell them for a profit. However, he didn't make much of a living, so he joined the army as a musician and served in Scotland under General Wade. But it wasn't long before he was back.

Sometime in the 1760s, the local authority decided to build a turnpike road between Harrogate and Boroughbridge, and Jack, being an astute businessman, asked for, and won, the right to build a three-mile stretch between Minskip and Fearnsby. This short contract started him on a 30-year career in road building, during which time he built many roads throughout Yorkshire and Lancashire. Amongst others, he laid the foundations for routes between Wakefield and Doncaster, Harrogate and Harewood Bridge, Knaresborough and Wetherby, and Huddersfield and Halifax. In Lancashire he instigated roads between Bury and Blackburn, and between Haslingdon and Accrington. Roads across the peaks and around the Buxton area were also laid and built by Blind Jack and his team. He learnt as he went along, and ultimately devised a road surface consisting of three layers: large stones, excavated road material, and a top layer of gravel. He was one of the first road builders to understand the importance and efficiency of road draining, and successfully devised a way of 'floating' the road surface on top of anything wet, such as a bog.

You may well wonder how a blind man could measure and devise these roads. The answer is that he used a wooden instrument called a 'viameter', which measured distances by means of a wheel. He took one of these and had it specially adapted in order to be able to 'read' it by touch.

After eventually building around 180 miles of road throughout Yorkshire and Lancashire, he died in 1810 at the age of 93, leaving behind a legacy of road building which would be remarkable for any man. The fact that Jack Metcalf was blind serves to show how truly extraordinary he actually was.

Did you know?

Roads and lanes with hardly any traffic are called 'C', 'D' and 'U' (Unclassified) roads. These can be numbered, but that's done mainly for the benefit of the local authorities, who are responsible for maintaining them. The numbering is arbitrary and usually doesn't appear on any public signage.

era of substantial road building. Engineers like John MacAdam and Thomas Telford started to experiment with different hard road surfaces. MacAdam's combination of tar and roadstone became the longstanding tarmacadam material that still paves our nation's roads today.

Of course, the toll roads weren't without their problems. Many travellers weren't happy to pay, and sometimes didn't, and often the trusts themselves were irresponsible, corrupt, or simply couldn't be bothered to maintain their roads properly. Despite the optimism that surrounded their birth, the Turnpike Trusts simply couldn't cover the country in a network of suitable and effective roads, and the last one closed for business in 1895.

Early road development

As the Turnpike Trusts came to an end at the close of the 19th century, and the era of coaches declined, the first automobiles began to emerge. As more cars and lorries started appearing in the late 1800s and early 1900s, it was clear that there was a real need for a better road system. However, although around 1,900 local authorities were concerned with highways, there was no 'big picture' – a national policy was needed to coordinate all roads across the country. Traffic was increasing rapidly and so the government scratched its head and decided that some roads should be 'A' roads and others 'B' roads, in other words some big and others small. They allotted money for this development via an Act of Parliament in 1919, and started building.

The 'Rules of the Road', a sort of early Highway Code, had already been created. The Locomotive Act of 1865 had decreed that all 'locomotive' vehicles should have three attendants – one to steer, another to stoke the engine, and, yes, one to walk 60 yards ahead with a red flag, telling the driver where he should stop. The speed limit at that time was set at 4mph. This Act thus became known as The Red Flag Act.

The Locomotive Act was refined in 1896, when lighter vehicles – those under three tons, that is – no longer needed a Red Flag, and the speed limit went up to a staggering 14mph. The Act also introduced the idea that any vehicle should stop when ordered to do so by a policeman or when they saw a horse.

Slowly but surely more and more roads were built across the country, and a network seemed to be emerging. In 1936 the Government put through the first Trunk Roads Act. This meant that, finally, overall control of the nation's main roads lay with the Minister of Transport. These numbered around 30 at the time, and their total mileage was about 4,500 miles. Minor roads still remained in the hands of local authorities, but from now on there would be consistency in types of road surface, treatment of bridges and the ultimate development of the motorway. Finally, in 1946, the then Labour Government set out its plan for a national network of quality roads.

The problem, of course, was that as the road network developed, so did the number of towns. As a result, going from A to B, now meant going via a developing town at C.

In 1948, an act to create 'Special Roads' – which were restricted to motorised traffic – was passed in parliament. This was the first step towards the motorway network as we know it. However, it wasn't until 1956 that the government actually got their act together. And so they began…

Their first idea was to build a huge road that would bypass a small town called Preston in the north-west of England. So they started building, cautiously and sparingly. It was opened in December 1958 by Prime Minister Harold Macmillan, and became the Preston Bypass (later to become part of the M6).

It was a roaring success – so much so that the builders completely underestimated how many cars would actually use it (nothing changes!), and after a hammering of high-speed traffic the UK's first motorway was closed for extensive maintenance.

Despite such hiccups the government realised that motorways were the way forward for Britain's ever-increasing motoring masses. So they got building miles and miles of road with better specifications and better capacity. The revolution continued, and in 1959 the first section of the M1 opened for business. It comprised almost 60 miles of six-lane motorway – the first in the country – and its first service area, the Watford Gap between Junctions 16 and 17, became a national tourist attraction! People drove miles to see this new idea, even taking picnics along to make a day of it. Additionally, and for the first time, the hard shoulders on this new section of motorway were specially strengthened.

The Watford Gap service area, immortalised in song by Roy Harper, still stands today – but it's never been anywhere near Watford. The reason why is surprisingly simple: the services were named for the tiny village of Watford, on the B5385 just outside Daventry. Watford Gap itself is a low pass through the Northampton uplands, once used by the Romans (who called it 'Watling Street') and now known as the A5. In fact this section of the M1 was partly built to relieve congestion along that bit of the A5 and also the nearby A6.

The M10 St Albans bypass and the M45 from Dunchurch to the M1 were also built at this time. The rest of the M1 developed in stages until 1999, and it now runs from Staples Corner in London, at the junction of the A406 North Circular Road, all the way to Junction 48 at Hook Moor, near Leeds. Its length is some 200 miles.

Early innovations
Road Signs
The Romans started this trend by using milestones between cities, some of which are still around today. In the 1770s the Turnpike Trusts became responsible for erecting signposts when people began paying to use their roads. When the railway and canal networks expanded and bridges became increasingly important, signs displaying weight restrictions

were introduced. Then, as the number of cars on the roads increased, the Motor Car Act of 1903 introduced legislation allowing local authorities to post signs regarding hazards and speed restrictions. In 1964 the Worboys report overhauled the entire road sign system, which remains much the same today. There's even a Transport font which was specifically created for road signage by Jock Kinneir and Margaret Calvert between 1957 and 1963, and has become known as 'the handwriting of Britain'. It's now used in many countries across the world as a standard type font for road signs.

Traffic lights

The first traffic lights in the UK were installed outside the Houses of Parliament on 10 December 1868, by the railway engineer J.P. Knight. They looked like railway signals then, and were powered by gas at night. Sadly, they exploded on 2 January 1869, injuring the policeman who was operating them.

> **Did you know?**
> *On average we spend two weeks of our lives waiting for traffic lights to change.*

It seems that traffic lights as we now know them, were invented in America, although there's some dispute about who exactly the inventor was. The first experimental automatic traffic lights in England were used in Princes Square in Wolverhampton in 1927.

Pedestrian crossings

These actually didn't come into use in the UK until 1949,

when they were painted blue and yellow. Earlier, in 1934, Leslie Hore-Belisha, the then Minister of Transport, had introduced the idea of a beacon to mark crossing points, and the large yellow ball on top of the black and white pole has been known as a Belisha Beacon ever since.

Roundabouts

The first roundabouts were developed in around 1922, and seem to have come from America. Gyratory systems were far more common in the early days of motoring in the UK, and one of the first these was Hyde Park Corner in central London, which came into use around 1927.

In my first ever traffic bulletin, many years ago, I mentioned the Shepherd and Flock Roundabout in Farnham, Surrey. In fact, this is not so much a roundabout, more a small village. It extends over ten acres and has 17 houses and a pub (The Shepherd and Flock), making it one of the largest roundabouts in the world. Its existence results from an anomaly of 1960s road planning.

Petrol pumps

The first roadside petrol pumps were installed in the USA in 1906, and the first drive-in petrol station with pumps on islands was built in Detroit in 1910 by the Central Oil Company. Britain's first roadside petrol station was opened in Shrewsbury in 1913, although pumps didn't come into general use in the UK until 1921. The first British self-service petrol pump opened for business in November 1961 at Southwark Bridge in London.

White lines
The first broken white line road markings were used on a 70-mile stretch of the A30/A38 in Devon in 1935. The first double white lines, indicating where drivers couldn't overtake, appeared in the centre of roads throughout Britain in 1957, following a European agreement.

Flyovers
The first British flyovers were on the Winchester bypass. They opened in 1939 at the junctions with the Alton and Alresford roads, and with the old A33 at Compton.

Motorway development

After the opening of the Preston Bypass in 1958 (now part of the M6 between Junctions 29 and 32), the initial period of calm on the road quickly gave way to usage by thousands of vehicles. Today, this eight-and-a-quarter mile stretch of road regularly carries around 140,000 vehicles per day, and that figure is rising.

In 1959, the Chiswick Flyover in West London was built. Although this was never intended to be a motorway as such, it was considered at the time to be a major road scheme. It now forms Junction 1 of the M4 motorway. It was intended to relieve congestion at the western end of the A4 Cromwell Road in West London, and the A30 Great West Road, which extends past Heathrow airport towards the south-west of England. It's completion meant that traffic could move much more freely to and from the west side of London without having to use what was then quite a complicated road system. This section of the M4 was quickly extended, eventually becoming the Slough and Langley Bypass, which is now the M4 between Junctions 1 and 5. Of course, this stretch of road eventually resulted in the entire M4 motorway, which was built in stages between 1961 and 1972, linking London to South Wales. In fact, the first toll bridge in the country was across the M4, now the M48, and was called the Severn crossing. It opened in September 1966.

At 230 miles the M6 is Britain's longest and, some would argue, most important motorway. Its construction doesn't seem to have followed any particular order – sections were built at various times between 1958 (the Preston Bypass) and 1972. The M6 across Shap, around Junction 39, is one of the most beautiful stretches of motorway anywhere in the country. And everyone knows about Spaghetti Junction – a mass of road-knitting at Junction 6. It looks far more complicated than

Did you know?

Believe it or not, there's such an organisation as the United Kingdom Roundabout Association. Their main aim is to promote safe driving and to raise awareness of all aspects of roundabouts, including general design and safety, and wildlife that may be living on them. Its founder, Kevin Beresford, came to prominence when he published a calendar showing all the roundabouts in Redditch, in the Midlands, and the society now meets on a regular basis. Sounds fun.

it is to drive around, although there was controversy at the time of its opening because of the amount of demolition required in the surrounding area. The junction covers 30 acres (12 hectares), serves 18 routes, and includes 2.5 miles (4km) of slip roads. But it only represents 0.6 miles (1km) of the M6 itself.

Between 1959 and 1961 a further seven motorways were opened, including the Maidstone Bypass, now part of the M20.

By 1966 the M1 and M6 were approaching their long-awaited completion, and at the end of that year it was possible to travel all the way from Birmingham to Lancaster by motorway, and most of the way from London to Leeds. By the end of the 1960s 1,000 miles of motorway had been completed throughout the UK. The government pledged to match that in the following decade. Motorways had arrived, and they were here to stay.

From then on motorways popped up everywhere. One of the biggest and most expensive was the M25, which circumvents London, built at a cost of £909 million (roughly £7.5 million per mile) between 1975 and 1986. Although a motorway, it actually starts and finishes on the A282, near the Dartford Crossing, and although it sometimes seems much longer it in fact stretches for only 118 miles. The section on the western side around Heathrow is considered to be one of the busiest stretches of motorway in the country. However, recent improvements along this stretch have made it into a six-lane highway and it's improved a bit. But try using it after 4 o'clock in the afternoon, especially on a Friday...

With the tarmac came the technology, and it developed

fast. Crash barriers became a permanent fixture on all routes, electronic matrix signs started popping up across the country, and quality and speed of building reached standards never seen before.

The oil crisis of the mid-1970s brought fresh problems. Road building began to slow down. Technical faults, changing specifications and strikes meant unfinished roads and unhappy drivers. The industrial development of the country, coupled with its rapid growth, simply wasn't matched by funding, and the road builders couldn't keep up. By the end of the decade, Government targets had not been met.

Britain's transport system needed a saviour before it ground to a halt. The change in attitude came in 1986, when Conservative Prime Minister Margaret Thatcher inspired a new-era of pro-roads policy, and the government declared that 'anyone aged 30 and on a bus is a failure'. Within a couple of years a white paper entitled 'Roads to Prosperity' was published, outlining plans to build hundreds of miles of new road. The paper didn't go though, and many of the roads weren't built, but the work had been done – attitudes had been changed, and the government pressed on with its roads. Thatcher personally opened the final section of M25 as a symbol of her support. Within a few weeks the road was running beyond its intended capacity. Again.

With the 1990s came New Labour, and road building slowed down. The government got behind the rail network as the means of transport for the country. In 2000 the very last motorway to be funded by the government was opened – the M60 in Manchester. For the first time since 1954, there were no motorways under construction. However, 2001 saw the birth of Britain's first tolled motorway route, the controversial M6 Toll Road, funded by a consortium of local companies.

Britain's motorised landscape has changed a lot since the 1950s. Attitudes have changed too. Although the excitement of the early days of discovery has now faded, and environmental concerns have become more and more important, we live in a country that counts on motorways as an essential part of its everyday work and life.

All in all there are now 2,201.88 miles of motorway across the whole of the United Kingdom. And that figure is still growing.

The longest motorway

As I've said, the M6 motorway is the longest motorway in the United Kingdom. Running from the M1's Junction 19 near Rugby, it passes near Coventry, through Birmingham, and past the major cities of Wolverhampton, Stoke-on-Trent, Manchester, Liverpool and Preston, to end north of Carlisle, close to the Scottish border. It's often referred to as the country's backbone, as it forms part of the central road corridor between London and Glasgow.

Very silly short motorways

Don't ask me why, but these motorways really do exist. I think in some cases they're genuine mistakes, in others the money just ran out. Whatever the reason, they are the runts of the litter!

The M10 runs for 2.75 miles off the M1 at Junction 7.

The M32 into Bristol runs for just over 4 miles.

The M67 in Lancashire, 5 miles long.

The M96 in Gloucestershire, at just a mile long is hardly a motorway at all really.

The M271 out of Southampton, only 2.5 miles long.

The M898 in Renfrewshire, 1 mile long.

The M41 West Cross Route in West London, just 0.7 miles long!

No motorways at all

Yes, believe it or not there really are still quite a large number of counties out there with no motorways at all...

Aberdeenshire	Denbighshire	Norfolk
Anglesey	Dorset	Orkney
Angus	Dumbartonshire	Peeblesshire
Argyllshire	East Lothian	Pembrokeshire
Banffshire	East Sussex	Radnorshire
Berwickshire	Flintshire	Ross-shire
Breconshire	Inverness-shire	Roxburghshire
Buteshire	Kincardineshire	Rutland
Caernarfonshire	Kirkcudbrightshire	Selkirkshire
Caithness	Merionethshire	Shetland
Cardiganshire	Montgomeryshire	Suffolk
Clackmannanshire	Morayshire	Sutherland
Cornwall	Nairnshire	Wigtownshire

The open road

We're so lucky in Britain that our A and B roads are among the most beautiful anywhere. My favourite way to drive is definitely off the beaten track, down windy, tree-filled lanes, through villages and along coastal routes where you can almost feel the water on your face. It's here that you really get a feeling of freedom and magic, uncluttered roads, and an old, unhurried way of life long gone. One of the things my current satnav can do is to take me to places via scenic routes I wouldn't otherwise have known about, and through it I've discovered all sorts of new places. I've driven thousands of miles, but some of the most stunning places have been unexpected – glorious surprises stumbled on by taking a wrong turn.

I found myself in the summer of 2007 driving across the roads of the Lake District. Here, it's hard to concentrate on actually driving because all you want to do is look at the stunning scenery, consisting of fells, lakes and beautiful countryside. The A595 running south of Whitehaven towards Barrow in Furness is a particularly beautiful route, as it meanders along the coast to one side and the Lake District National Park on the other. It was also here that I attempted a difficult route too, the Hardknott Pass. This single-track road connecting Ambleside to Eskdale runs through the most beautiful scenery I've ever seen, but negotiating a hairpin bend at 33 degrees, in the rain, was also one of the most terrifying experiences of my life!

These are the joys of driving and are utterly different to the daily commute, the slog along the motorway, when we forget how wonderful or challenging driving can be.

If you find yourself driving along a dead straight road it was probably built by those Romans to connect their military bases and settlements, though some were built later as parish boundaries. More bendy, winding roads are usually like that because they have adapted to the surrounding countryside, avoiding such things as houses, streams and the like.

Built initially for horses and carts, the narrowest roads in Britain are only 12ft wide, which is just enough nowadays to allow a couple of cars to pass each other. These can be dangerous places for less experienced drivers, some of whom still race along as if they were driving on the M1. It's likely that such roads have never been widened because there's simply not enough traffic to justify it. These tiny roads are redolent of the history of our country and in my eyes remain beautiful. Just use them slowly.

In a study sponsored by Dunlop in 2005, a panel of racing drivers and motoring journalists decided that the road from Moffat to Selkirk in Scotland was the most beautiful in the country. They described this stretch of the A708 as 'an excellent alternative to the grid-locked motorway and deserving of national acclaim'. In addition, they felt that 'the ten-mile route following the beautiful St Mary's Loch is a particular highlight and worth the detour alone.' An eight-mile stretch of the A6024 between the Snake Pass and Holmfirth in West Yorkshire came second, and in third place was the road between Hardknott and Wynrose Pass in Cumbria. Also making the final list was the A481 in Wales, the B296 outside Oxted in Kent, and the B660 from Peterborough to the A14. Of course, this is the opinion of a panel, albeit an expert one, and you may have your own favourites. Some of the most beautiful roads I know include those on the Isles of Skye and Mull, the coastal route south of Bodmin, in Cornwall, and some of the narrow roads of Sussex.

Spooky roads

I was sitting one evening with my brother, Bill, who recounted an experience he'd had one night many years ago. He was on the B3272, a road which connects Eversley to Yateley, and it was just after midnight. As he walked home, he was aware that two figures on the other side of the road were having a confrontation. As he glanced across to see what all the fuss was about, he noticed that the men were wearing long, dark cloaks and seemed incredibly tall, with hats that seemed to stretch well above ground level. Not wanting to get involved, he looked away, but moments later, when he looked back, they had completely disappeared. We both came to the conclusion that he may have seen something, well, at best odd, and at most, ghostly. Their height and demeanour indicated that they may have been on horses, possibly highwaymen, and having a dispute of some sort. Indeed, research shows that this area was notorious for robberies of all kinds during the eighteenth century, to the point where coaches and travellers would avoid the area altogether.

This got me thinking: are there spooky happenings on roads across the country? Tarmac, one of Britain's largest road contractors, published a survey in 2006 and they came to some startling conclusions. It would appear that the M6 is one of the spookiest roads in Britain, where more sightings were reported than any other road in the country. Indeed, the survey showed that over 45 per cent of drivers have seen something out of the ordinary, which they put down to a supernatural phenomenon of some sort; roman soldiers, a 'lone woman' and old modes of transport were all reported, including trains. Vehicles are often reported as being on the same side of the road, but travelling directly towards a driver, then suddenly disappearing.

All of the following roads were cited as spooky, with drivers reporting specific experiences of ghosts, vehicles and other phenomena. According to the Tarmac survey, the top ten spooky roads are:

1. M6
2. The A9 in the Highlands, Scotland
3. Platt Lane, in the Leigh area of Manchester
4. Great Yarmouth – along the High Street and Suffield Road
5. Gloucester Drive, in Finsbury Park, North London
6. The B4293 at Devauden, north of Chepstow
7. Cornwall; the B3314 near Tintagel
8. Highlands, Loch Dornoch, on the east coast of Scotland
9. Doncaster, on the B1403 known as the Canon Ball Run
10. Birmingham, along Drews Lane, Ward End

And here are some of the drivers' accounts:

M6, near Knutsford: Robert Teese, Knutsford. Robert tells his story, saying, 'I was driving back home alone one night and there was a clump of mist on the road ahead. As I drove on, it got bigger and formed a shape – like a train I thought at first. I blinked and could still see it. Then as it got closer, I realised it was a lorry, coming straight towards me on the wrong side of the road. It was very realistic, just a bright glowing white HGV. I remember looking in my mirror and thinking I wonder if the car behind me can see it, but I could only see small headlights, so they were far away. Then as it got closer, it didn't disappear, it kept coming for me. I slowed right down and closed my eyes – this sounds stupid now but I did! I moved into the slow lane and the lorry came right by me, careering down the M6 the wrong way and I winced as it felt like it was going to rip off one side of my car. But I looked in my rear mirror straight after – I was sweating and my palms couldn't hold the steering wheel – there was nothing, absolutely nothing. I didn't imagine it, I know I didn't, but I've never really told anyone else about it apart from my wife.'

A9 travelling north from Pitlochry towards Newtonmor: Lizzie Lane from the Isle of Arran says: 'My husband was driving, with me in the passenger seat and my 12-year-old son was in the back. We all witnessed the scene – it was completely awesome. Like seeing through time, we saw a coach like one the Queen uses on state occasions. It was being pulled by immaculately groomed white horses. Everything was illuminated in the most perfect glittering detail – the golden ornate coach, coachmen, white wigs, white stockings, knee length breeches and embroidered jackets. At first I thought I must be seeing a film set except there were no other people around and I realised they would never be filming at such a dangerous location. The coach was at the side of the road, facing into the oncoming traffic. I soon realised that no one else could possibly be seeing what we were. As we drove by we all turned our heads to look back, although my husband did not get the chance to see as much as my son and I did. However, he saw enough to leave him convinced. He used to be a total sceptic of such things, but now he's a complete convert.'

B4293 at Devauden, north of Chepstow: Dean Llewellyn from Ludlow tells his story: 'My wife, Sue, was travelling home alone to Abergavenny late at night on very quiet country roads. The B4293 is a very twisty wooded route. After she passed through Devauden, she approached a severe bend in the road. From beside her she heard a soft, calm voice tell her to stop. Taken aback she slowed and pulled onto the side of the grass verge. Almost immediately a car came towards her with no lights on, travelling at a very high speed and on the wrong side of the road. Had she not pulled over she would have had a serious accident. Sue searched the car and the roadside for any sign of her 'guardian' but found no one...'

Doncaster, just off B1403: Lynne Shaw from Retford says: 'It was September last year and there was a storm. My boyfriend convinced me to go out to the top of Gringley on the Hill and watch it from a distance. After watching for a while, we moved onto a lane called The Cannon Ball Run. I sat with my window right down but facing toward the driver's seat looking out that window at the storm. We had the headlights on and suddenly I saw a shadow. I turned around, not thinking anything of it, but to my amazement I saw a soldier! You could see his hat and his shiny buttons on his military jacket all the way up to his neck. He wasn't looking at us, he was marching straight past. My boyfriend was really scared and started the engine, but I grabbed his arm and told him to wait. The soldier walked in front of the car and then disappeared in the headlights. Never at any moment did I feel frightened or threatened. The pure detail in his outfit was amazing, not like on movies where you can see through a ghost. It was a great but chilling experience!'

So next time you see something strange, don't panic. They're just being friendly...

I think a smaller wheel would be better . . .

Chapter Four

A Brief History of Cars and Trucks

'If we continue to develop our technology
without wisdom or prudence, our servant
may prove to be our executioner.'
Omar N. Bradley

Stagecoach travel reached its peak in 1830 with 30,000 people regularly using the roads, but by the mid-1800s this figure was on its way down. A faster, more efficient and altogether more attractive form of transport had arrived: the railway.

The history of railways can be traced back over half a millennium, but their rebirth in modern form commenced in 1803 with arguably the world's first public railway – although back then it was horse-drawn. This railway in South London was operated by the Surrey Iron Railway company and ran between Wandsworth and Croydon via Mitcham. This was a bit like a turnpike road in terms of ownership, allowing anyone to use a vehicle on it provided they paid a toll. There were no official routes or regular services.

In the 1820s railways hit the mainstream, and suddenly became useful for the public transportation of goods. The first, in 1825, was the Stockton and Darlington Railway, which enabled local collieries to transport their coal to the docks. These eventually became powered by locomotive, and it was from here that railways evolved into the timetabled passenger trains that we know today.

Railways continued to go from strength to strength and, of course, they are still with us, but at the same time that the railways were developing so was the car – and another enduring form of transport was also being born: the bicycle.

The bicycle

The first bike – of a sort – was invented by Baron von Drais in around 1817. However, this machine, with tiny little wheels, required you to push yourself along the ground using your own feet, a bit like a scooter, as there were no pedals. It was known as the Hobby Horse. Scooters have now become popular again, and can be seen ferrying businessmen, office workers and others through busy cities.

Pedals finally appeared in 1865, when they were applied to a front wheel, and the boneshaker, or velocipede, was born. Five years later, metal became the material of choice for bicycle construction, and with this development came the high wheel bicycle, or penny farthing. Popular with Britain's men in the 1880s, the disproportionately larger front wheel had a rubber rim, to match a baby wheel at the back, not exactly the cushioned, gripped tyres of today's mountain bikes, but a step in the right direction.

While men risked their necks on the high wheel bicycle,

women went for the slightly more practical high wheel tricycle, that is, a bike with three separate wheels; I suppose it seemed safer. It was also deemed 'more elegant'. But by the turn of

the 20th century bikes were starting to shape up into the form we know and love today. By this time cycles with two wheels of the same size had become the norm. Chains and gears began to develop, and bicycles became an ever-more important form of transport in the modern world. The second half of the century saw bikes become more and more sophisticated. Gears became more intricate, hi-tech materials were developed so that frames got steadily lighter, and suspension arrived on the scene. Racing bikes pushed the boundaries even further.

Despite a dip in the use of bikes in the 1980s and 1990s, they're now back in vogue with a vengeance. In this greener, more environmentally friendly world, bikes are seen not only as a way to stay fit, but also as a contribution towards saving the planet. Pedal-power has never been more fashionable.

What's that on the road?
Early car development

Beginnings

The first car can be traced back to 1769, and Nicholas Cugnot's experimentations. Cugnot, a designer and engineer, initially developed an engine that was driven by steam. It travelled at walking pace, and could carry about four passengers. A year later he came up with the 'Fardier', another steam-powered vehicle which consisted of a wooden chassis sitting on a boiler at the front. Behind this chassis was a seat and a brake pedal. There was no bodywork, so protection from the weather – and, indeed, other people – was non-existent.

1860

After a gap of around 100 years, along comes Belgian-born Frenchman, Jean-Joseph Etienne Lenoir, who patented the first successful internal combustion engine in 1860. This was what was known as a 'two-stroke' engine, and ran on coal gas; the gas was drawn into a cylinder by a piston and ignited halfway through the stroke, which forced the other stroke to finish off.

1876

Learning of Lenoir's two-stroke gas-driven internal combustion engine, Nikolaus Otto started a workshop in Deutz near Cologne, where, supported by his partner Langen, he created an engine that improved on it. The four-stroke Otto engine appeared in 1876, and a large number were produced under the patent of Otto and Langen. It was, however, their chief designer and engineer Gottlieb Daimler who carried out much of the development work, and substantial credit for the success of their engines is due to him. However, he became frustrated with the team, and when he began to look at petrol rather than gas to power their engines they fired him. This was probably the best thing that ever happened to him. He set up another company and eventually developed a more powerful engine that could run at 700rpm, which he attached to a wooden frame.

1885

The first real automobile, powered by a four-stroke gas-fired Otto internal combustion engine, was built by Karl Benz in 1885. It was granted a patent the following year, and France, America and Britain quickly got in on the act.

1886

After Daimler left Otto he set up an independent company with a partner, Wilhelm Maybach, and they designed the first petrol engine in 1883. In 1885 he fitted one to a bicycle and created the prototype of the present-day motorcycle, and a year later fitted another to a horse-carriage to create the first four-wheeled motor car in history.

1891

Two Frenchmen, Emile Levassor and René Panhard, took car design a step further when they built a vehicle with the engine in front. The car consisted of a Daimler engine, a pedal-operated clutch, a change-speed gearbox, which drove the rear axle, a front radiator, and a wooden ladder chassis.

This became the forerunner of the modern-day car.

One of the biggest problems facing earlier motor car developers was what to call their vehicles. Some suggestions were horseless carriage, autobain, automobile carriage, automatic carriage, self-propelled carriage, motocycle and autocar. However, in 1891 British engineer Frederick R. Simms settled on 'motor car', although in Europe and America they called the same thing an 'automobile'. Simms also coined the word 'petrol' at around the same time. He had become aware that drivers were slightly worried about using inflammable petroleum fuel, so he adopted this neutral-sounding French word to help allay their fears. But in America they went their own way; their term for motor fuel has always been gasoline.

1893

Enter the United States! Charles and Frank Duryea were two bicycle makers who saw a gasoline engine at the Ohio State Fair in 1886, and were so sure they could make something of it, that by 1893 they had built an engine-driven carriage

Did you know?

The M62 is the UK's highest motorway, reaching 372m (1,220ft) above sea level near the Pennine Way Footbridge by Junction 22. The M6 at Shap, near Junction 39, is not only one of the most beautiful stretches of motorway, but at 370m (1,214ft) is another of the highest.

which became the first car in the US to be commercially sold. They had built and sold 13 by 1896.

1901

An American named Ransome Elic Olds set up a factory in Detroit to mass produce cars and called the company Oldsmobile. He was the first person to introduce assembly line production. However, the factory burned down before production began, and the only prototype to survive was the Oldsmobile Gas Buggy, a single-cylinder vehicle which proved highly successful and sold in large numbers. Olds eventually left the company to set up another, far less successful venture. The Oldsmobile company merged with Buick in 1908, which eventually led to the formation of General Motors.

What's that on the road?
Early truck development

1769

Cugnot, who had developed the steam engine in 1769, seems to have also built the first truck at around the same time. This was a steam-powered *fardier à vapour* (steam wagon), which could apparently pull four tonnes and travel at 4mph. In 1771 this vehicle ran into a wall, thus possibly becoming the first motor accident in history! The roads at the time, however, were not suitable for such large vehicles, and it wasn't until the mid-1800s that trucks started appearing regularly. Steam-powered trucks remained in use right up until the start of the First World War, usually transporting goods between factories and railway stations.

1881

The first semi-trailer lorry (without a front axle) arrived in 1881 on the back of a de Dion steam tractor. De Dion was a French aristocrat who had pioneered steam-powered engines in the 1880s. His trucks were still sold in France and the USA until the turn of the 20th century.

1895

It was Karl Benz who in 1895 designed and built the first truck to use an internal combustion engine. Later that year he also developed the first bus using this engine.

1898

Daimler took on the internal combustion engine to build a range of trucks in 1898, with Peugeot and Renault following suit. Most of them were built for pretty short journeys and could only carry about 2,000kg.

1914

By the outbreak of the First World War trucks could carry loads of up to 25,000kg, and by 1914 25,000 trucks a year were being manufactured in the United States alone. The groundwork had been done.

After the war specific types of truck were developed, with pneumatic tyres (replacing the original solid rubber type), power brakes, closed cabs and electric starters.

Despite its invention in the 19th century, the diesel engine didn't become common in trucks until the 1920s, or in the US until the 1970s.

Early innovations

Airbags

It may come as a surprise that rudimentary patents for airbags go back to the 1950s. German inventor Walter Linderer's airbag, based on a compressed air system, was released either by bumper contact, or deliberately by the driver.

It wasn't until 1971 that airbags exploded, as it were, into mainstream car production, when Ford built an experimental airbag fleet. In 1973 the Oldsmobile Tornado was the first car fitted with airbags intended for sale to the public and by the 1990s they had become quite common. Frontal bags were supplemented by side-impact and passenger bags, and now it's hard to imagine a world without them.

Air conditioning

When cars were first built they were not particularly pleasant to drive in, particularly in extreme weather. The poor driver was cold in the winter, and hot in the summer (there's not much of a breeze at 15mph!). The first attempts at air conditioning started with vents in the floor, but these let in dust and dirt as well as cool air. So in 1884 William Whiteley started experimenting with blocks of ice and fans to blow cold air into the car. The next logical step was an evaporating cooling system, invented by a company

> **Did you know?**
>
> *Sally has an Eddie Stobart lorry named after her, so if you see the Sally B trundling the roads of Britain, give her a cheery wave!*

called Nash, where air passed over a body of water thus lowering its temperature.

But the first car with actual air conditioning was the 1939 Packard, which used a large evaporator or 'cooling coil' so big that it took up the whole boot. Packard marketed the system with the slogan 'Forget the heat this summer in the only air-conditioned car in the world!'

Not to be outdone, Cadillac quickly followed suit and produced 300 air-conditioned cars. The only problem was that you couldn't turn them off! The air conditioning came on with the engine, and wouldn't switch off until the engine had switched off too. So the next step was a control system, which was developed after the Second World War. By 1954 air conditioning was complete, consisting of a two-cylinder reciprocating compressor and an all-brazed condenser. However, it didn't become standard equipment in the US until the late 1970s and early 1980s (1990s in the UK), since when most cars have had air conditioning fitted as a matter of course.

Hah Hah Hah!

A man is driving along in a thunderstorm. His windscreen wiper breaks off, so he stops at a garage to get another one:
'Excuse me, could you give me a windscreen wiper for my Audi?'
The shopkeeper answers, 'Absolutely – that sounds like a good deal to me.'

Number plates

The very first car number plates were issued in France in 1893, by their police force. They became standard in the UK at the start of the road taxation system, when all vehicles required a number, and plate, to register them for legal use.

Seatbelts

The first US patent for automobile seatbelts was issued to Edward J. Claghorn of New York on 10 February 1885. They were described as 'designed to be applied to the person, and provided with hooks and other attachments for securing the person to a fixed object.'

Swede Nils Bohlin invented the three-point seatbelt which is now a standard safety device in most cars. His lap-and-shoulder belt was introduced by Volvo in 1959.

By 1965 belts for the front seats of cars were compulsory throughout Europe, and by the time Jimmy Saville started his 'Clunk Click' ads in the 1970s we all knew that they were here to stay.

Child restraints

The first children's car seats were invented in 1921, following the introduction of Henry Ford's Model T. However, they were very different from today's. The earliest versions were essentially sacks with drawstrings attached to the back seat. In 1978 Tennessee became the first American state to make child safety seat use a legal requirement. UK law changed in September 2006, making child seats compulsory for all children up to age 12 or 135cm tall.

Power steering
In the 1920s, Francis W. Davis was the chief engineer of the truck division of the Pierce Arrow Motor Car Company, based in Buffalo, New York. He saw first-hand how hard it was to steer heavy vehicles. He therefore left his job and rented a small engineering shop in Waltham, Massachusetts, where he developed an hydraulic power steering system that ultimately led to power steering. Power steering became commercially available by 1951.

Sunshine roofs
The first sliding sunroof was fitted on a 40/50hp Rolls Royce 'Prince Jacques' limousine in Paris in 1913. The first electric sunroof appeared in Cadillacs in 1969.

Car mirrors
Rear-view mirrors only became compulsory on cars in Britain on 1 January 1932.

The ladies were there too...
Windscreen wipers
During a trip to New York a woman named Mary Anderson noticed that streetcar drivers had to open their cab windows when it rained in order to see. This got her thinking, and in November 1903 she was granted the first patent for a car window-cleaning device. She invented a swinging arm mechanism with a rubber blade, operated by the driver from within the vehicle via a lever. This was able to clean snow, rain, or sleet off the windscreen. Wipers became standard

equipment on all American cars by 1916. Wipers were first patented in the UK in 1911.

Another woman, Charlotte Bridgwood, invented the first automatic windshield wiper. As president of the Bridgwood Manufacturing Company of New York, she patented her electric roller-based windshield wiper (called the 'Storm Windshield Cleaner') in 1917. However, her product was not a commercial success.

An English woman, Dorothy Levitt, wrote a small book in 1909 entitled *The Woman and the Car*. She advised all women drivers to carry a mirror with a handle in the side pocket of the car so that they could repair their complexion after a drive, and use it 'to occasionally hold up to see what is behind you'. She also advised women to carry a small revolver at all times!

During the 1930s Helen Blair Bartlett developed new insulations for spark plugs. A geologist by training, her knowledge of petrology and mineralogy was critical in the development of innovative uses of ceramics containing alumina, a material known for its high hardness and wear resistance.

The car and its innovations gave women ample opportunity to invent. In the USA in 1923, of the 345 inventions listed under 'Transportation' in the *Women's Bureau Bulletin* number 28, about half were related to automobiles and another 25 concerned traffic signals and turn indicators. Among these inventions were a carburettor, a clutch mechanism, and a starting mechanism.

Bumper to bumper

Bumper stickers are meant to be placed on the bumper of your car, but can, of course, be placed just about anywhere. No one knows exactly where and when they originated, but it's been suggested that they have been around since before the Second World War. After that, creative people used them to further their political agendas and campaigns. This began in America, where they're still an important form of political propaganda during elections. In the 1970s and 1980s they began to push the boundaries of stating political preference. As well as signifying membership of political parties, clubs and societies they began to make statements, apparently quoting the thoughts of the driver inside. From the witty to the insulting, the philosophical to the inquisitive, bumper stickers became an art form in their own right.

From the US they made their way to Britain, where – although they're rarely used as political devices – they've become just as popular.

By the 1990s advertising execs had realised they were missing a trick. Bumper stickers are highly visible, so today they're widely used for advertisements, with some companies even offering to match car owners to the advertisers willing to pay for the ad. Unlike other advertising media such as newspapers and television, bumper stickers reach a wide and diverse audience. On any American highway today you'll see everything from fast food to Viagra advertised on the bumpers of family cars. Companies and sports organisations even make use of bumper stickers to promote famous people.

Around the world

Australian ute (utility pickup truck) enthusiasts tend to have an obsession with bumper stickers, often covering the entire rear window of their ute. The truck with the greatest variety of stickers is often the deciding factor in many Ute Muster 'Beaut Ute' competitions.

In Israel, one of the most popular songs of all time is *Shirat Hastiker* ('The Sticker Song') by Hadag Naschash, the words of which consist entirely of bumper sticker slogans.

My favourite bumper slogans

A real gentleman wouldn't stare at my stickers.

If you can read this, I've lost my trailer.

So many cats, so few recipes

Why do they call it rush hour?

My other car is also rubbish.

If you ate pasta and anti-pasta, would you still be hungry?

There are three kinds of people: those who can count and those who can't

Driver carries no cash: he's married.

Well, this day was a total waste of makeup.

It's lonely at the top, but you eat better.

That car needs a clean . . .

Chapter Five

Sally's Cars

*'Everything in life is somewhere else and you
get there in a car.'*
E.B. White

I took my first driving lessons in Paddington, west London. It was scary at the time, but in retrospect it was a great place to learn, because if you can drive around Paddington you can drive anywhere. My instructor was a weird man. He always had a riding crop with him in the car, because, he said, he was learning to ride a horse. He used to tap me on the knee with it whenever I made a mistake, until I asked him, please, to stop doing that. I suspect he rather enjoyed it, and I should have complained more, but at 17 I didn't know much, so I kept quiet.

I passed my test first time. I remember I wore a green dress, rather short, and just as we were setting off I saw that the rear window was misted up. Trying to be as safety conscious as possible, I asked if it could be cleaned before I set off. The examiner said that I could do it myself, so I turned around in the driving seat, leant over with a cloth – and exposed my entire backside. No wonder I passed. The poor man has probably never recovered.

I really learned about driving in my first car (named Esmeralda, you'll recall), a Hillman Imp. They were strange little cars with an engine made of aluminium. This was at the back of the car, with the boot at the front, which meant that when I got my next car I frequently forgot and tried to put luggage in the engine and oil in the boot. I once stopped at a garage on the A316 in Twickenham to top up with water. Esmeralda's cap was at such an angle that it pointed directly towards you, and when I undid it boiling water spurted out on to my arm. I was quickly whisked to hospital, where I was treated for first degree burns. My freckles have never come back. (Top tip: *never* check the water in your car when you've been driving; always wait for the engine to cool down.)

I drove everywhere in Esmeralda. I guess I had the same sense of sudden freedom that my dad's generation had during the heyday of the car, when suddenly you could travel anywhere you wanted, to places that were inaccessible by any other means. I had my first breakdown in this little thing, outside the Iranian Embassy in London. I hadn't got a clue what to do, so walked into the embassy to ask for help. They were extremely pleasant, and pointed me to a large, ornate room to sit whilst they said they'd phone for help. In retrospect, it's likely they simply watched me sitting there, checked out my car and decided I was genuine. With the innocence of youth, I thought they were being kind. They probably were, but fortunately I didn't try to steal the silver.

I also had my first scrape in Esmeralda. Travelling through the narrow streets of Wandsworth, south London, one day, I saw a lorry coming towards me and thought I could squeeze past him. I couldn't, and Esmeralda got scraped, or sideswiped, all down the driver's side. Of course, the trucker blamed me, and he was probably right; but I didn't really listen, I was too preoccupied with how sad my little Imp looked.

It was also in this car that I discovered the roads of Britain. She was only a small thing with an 875cc engine, but I pummelled her. We drove to Land's End, to Scotland, to East Anglia – everywhere. I snogged in her, cried in her, laughed in her, and above all I loved her. Really. Like a best friend. It was the first time I discovered how easy it is to get attached to vehicles, to these mounds of metal and rubber. I know now from speaking to drivers across the country that this is a familiar and common feeling. Drivers who spend hours every day in a particular vehicle come to love it, and in a way it becomes a part of you. I've never felt the same about any car I've had since Esmeralda, and I hope that wherever she is she's happy, and that maybe some of her parts survive!

Did you know?

If you're in a car when lightning strikes, you're generally safe. This is due to the Faraday effect by which the electricity dissipates over the area of the car. There would be a potential difference – Pd or V (volts) – between different points across the area of, say, the roof, for example. This effect causes circles of electricity over the 'cage' of the car.

From Esmeralda I graduated to an Austin 1100, which had been my mum's but was no longer wanted. She took over my beloved Imp's parking space outside my bed-sit and became a good friend. She also had something I'd not had before – a radio with a tape player! Tragedy struck one night, though: I came down in the morning to find my car not there. She had simply vanished. I phoned the police, who got back to me soon afterwards to say she had been found at the bottom of my road. I went to find her, and she was in a bit of a state. The thieves had just taken her down the road, then tried to remove the radio. They couldn't, so there were wires and paraphernalia all over the place – not to mention broken windows and doors. I drove back home in tears, sorry to see her so sad. Going through the mess when I got back I found a note which read 'This car is crap'. Yeah, but it was *my* crap. Cheeky bastards.

I remember driving her to Scotland one year. I picked up a boyfriend in Coventry on the way, and then headed north. It was the first time I ever negotiated Spaghetti Junction, but we sailed through it effortlessly. When we finally arrived in Scotland we camped on a lot of little islands, which meant taking the car on to some of the smallest ferries I'd ever seen. We got stuck getting off one, and the entire crew had to push us to safety on the jetty. One night we camped alongside a beautiful loch on the Isle of Mull. It was deserted, and we had a romantic night in front of a burning fire. However, the next morning we were woken by the sounds of strange songs, and peeked out from the tent to find ourselves surrounded by a troop of Boy Scouts. The car was stuck in amongst them, looking as startled as us.

She also smelt of garlic. One day, driving to work, I found myself waiting at a roundabout on a slight upwards incline, behind a lorry carrying all sorts of vegetables. As he took off a massive bag of garlic fell into the road. I stopped, picked it up and threw it into the back of the car, intending to catch him up and hand it back. But he disappeared in the London traffic, so I kept it. I spent all day at work giving out cloves of garlic and telling everyone that they'd fallen off the back of a lorry. Of course, no one believed me. But some of it had escaped into my car without me knowing, and the smell eventually permeated into the carpets and the seats. It wasn't, therefore, a great car for pulling.

I suppose my first proper grown-up car was a Ford Escort Mark III. I bought it just after I got married and Harry was born. It was the first four-door car I had ever owned, so it really did feel posh. Harry would sit in his baby seat alongside me, and together we would wander the streets of London, shopping and going to parks. As he got older he sat in the seat at the back, and began to love his car. When he was two years old we moved abroad and on the first day in our new country a friend gave us a lift in his own Ford Escort. When Harry saw the Ford logo in the middle of the steering wheel he immediately said 'My car!' I'd had no idea he was going to become as attached to his cars as I was!

Then there was the Fiat Panda, the one with the canvas roof that you can roll back – it's almost a convertible, but not quite. I bought it because it was cheap, and the roof, I thought, gave it character. It also turned out to be extremely

The world's largest car park is in a mall in Edmonton, Alberta: it has spaces for 20,000 cars, with an overflow park for another 10,000.

useful, because in the wink of an eye you got a massive hole in the roof so that you could transport all manner of things. I remember buying a Christmas tree one year and driving it all the way home sticking through the roof. It looked as if I'd inadvertently driven through a forest and come out with a free tree.

One day in the summer, Harry and I were driving home after school with the roof down, singing. We found ourselves driving through roadworks when, all of a sudden, and at the very moment we were driving through them, one of the workmen hit a mains water pipe and it exploded. We were suddenly drenched. It was as if a large cloud had burst just above us. After the initial shock we couldn't stop laughing until we arrived home soaking wet. So now, when I talk about delays because of a burst water main, I really do know what I'm talking about.

Then there was the Volvo. It was the sporty 470 model, and I named her Doris. She was the nearest thing to a sports car I ever owned. I bought her on HP, and she was the first car I bought just for *me*. It even had a 'computer', which really wasn't one at all, but kept you abreast of all sorts of information like petrol consumption, oil level and mileage. Very posh. At the time I bought her I was working for GLR, and doing my broadcasts from Scotland Yard, so I was using the Scotland Yard car park. For security reasons we had to leave our ignition keys in the car, I suppose so that they could be moved in an emergency.

One day Doris wouldn't start. In a panic, I managed to get a hire car, which turned out to be a Ford Escort. I raced into work, parked it up, left the keys in the ignition, did my shift, went back to the car park, got in the car, and drove it back to the car hire company. Of course, they needed to inspect it for any damage and came outside to have a look. After a while they said 'It's not our car.' 'Yes it is!' I insisted. But the registration was definitely different. On closer examination, the glovebox wasn't a glovebox at all but housed some complicated radio equipment including a walkie-talkie. It turns out I'd parked next to an unmarked police car, exactly the same model and colour, and had driven it an hour down the M3. Oops.

After Doris came a Ford Focus. This one was only a year old, so became the newest car I ever bought. It was a practical but ultimately unexciting car. After I'd had it about a year, I was driving to work one day when I realised I was low on oil. I stopped at a garage, and pumped a couple of cans into it. As soon as I drove off, I looked in my rear view mirror and couldn't see a thing for smoke. I'd put about six times too much oil in and it was as if I was driving in front of a cloud. I pulled over on to the hard shoulder and called the RAC. Their patrolman took me off the motorway and drained all the oil out. It was the only time I ever missed a broadcast at Radio 2, and Steve Wright had to read out what would have been my first bulletin. He didn't even shout at me.

Romantic times on the road

OK, I admit it. My first romantic liaison, as it were, was in the back of a Mini. It was cramped, and I remember the bloke saying afterwards that we could grow a nice crop of tomatoes in the heat that had been generated. But this experience is by no means unique, and most of us have canoodled in a car at some time or other.

About two and a half million copies of Mills and Boon books were pulped and used to help with the top layer of the M6 Toll Road, near Birmingham. According to contractors Tarmac, this pulp helps to hold the tarmac and asphalt in place. They report that for every mile of motorway approximately 45,000 books were needed. So if you start to feel particularly romantic when you use the M6 Toll Road, it's because you're driving over a lot of romantic heroines and heroes who could be getting up to all sorts underneath you.

In a Microsoft poll in 2001 the M4 and M5 were voted the sexiest roads, with the best parking areas, services and grass verges – all, presumably, good snogging territory. The same survey cited an incident where a motorist helped change the tyre of a young lady in tears on the M1. They started a romance and he eventually proposed. She accepted and they are now married.

Another couple rekindled their romance after a gap of four years when they spotted each other in a traffic jam on the M40. They stopped at the next roadside services, and they too are now married.

In a survey conducted by the RAC Foundation, the following drivers were declared top of the romance table and logged their love lives as follows:

BMW drivers – 2.2 times a week
Audi drivers – 2.1 times a week
Mini drivers – 2.1 times a week
Drivers of Italian cars – 2 times a week
Volkswagen drivers – 1.9 times a week

There are now many websites that allow you to match up with drivers on the road. Once registered with these dating services, you usually receive a bumper sticker displaying your availability to all and sundry. If you're spotted, you can then be traced via a phone number and have an eyeball, as it were.

Rubber knickers

Chapter Six

Sally on Traffic

'*The car has become the carapace,*
the protective and aggressive shell,
of urban and suburban man.'
Marshall McLuhan

As I've already said, the roads in the UK are amongst the most beautiful in the world. And, according to the Highways Agency, they continue to be among the safest in Europe, despite carrying more traffic. Off the motorway, though, our A roads can be more hazardous. Here there are lower design standards, more junctions, fewer hard shoulders, and bigger speed differentials. All these factors contribute to roads off the motorway having higher casualty rates. Things such as cyclists, pedestrians, zebra crossings, traffic lights, roadworks and separate lanes for turning are hazards not encountered on motorways, thus creating potential for accidents almost everywhere. The RAC says the most accidents happen on urban roads, followed by rural roads, and finally dual carriageways.

Trunk and A roads

Although not all of us like to drive on motorways, if we drive at all then by default we have to drive on the rest of the road system. This includes major trunk routes, dual carriageways, city roads and small B roads. All of these are likely to be just as busy as motorways – in other words, there's just as likely to be a jam on the A11 going out of London on a Friday night as there is at the same time on the M11. And the frustrations can be exactly the same. Driving on these roads, though, is very different: breakdowns and accidents can have far more impact on the pace of traffic because often there's no hard shoulder to shift things on to, and emergency vehicles can often take longer to reach the scene. So the impact on congestion in general can be far worse. According to research from the Highways Agency, accidents on non-built-up roads are more likely to result in fatal or serious injuries and to involve three or more vehicles.

City driving and horns

Many of us, me included, don't like driving in big cities. They can be scary, inhospitable places, particularly if you're unfamiliar with the city, and if you dare to lose your way or show any hesitation at all you're likely to be screamed at. Nowadays, more people than ever drive on their horns: at the slightest mistake, the person behind you lets out an almighty and impatient beep, trying to make you understand that whatever you're doing is utterly unacceptable to them. This is particularly true in towns and cities where the local drivers feel comfortable, safe and at home. You're the idiot intruder, and in their territory. But this behaviour only increases levels of nervousness and fear, making you far more likely to make a mistake. Just remember, the impatient ones behind you are the people who think they know what they're doing, where they're going, and are the world's most wonderful drivers. Let them beep, and don't let their aggressive behaviour get to you. That's what they want, and by ignoring their horn or their verbal taunts you're the winner and are far more likely to have a safe journey.

Beeping horns is one of my pet peeves. You'd never know it, but it's actually still illegal to use your horn after 11:00 at night, a law flouted by almost everyone in the country and hardly ever enforced. The people who use their horn like a waving shotgun are the same ones who listen to music in their car so loudly that it sometimes feels as if they're having a party in your bedroom as they cruise by. They love the music, so they assume you must too – it's a way to show off, really. I don't think I've ever heard a beautiful classical piece of music being blasted out from one of these vehicles; it's always some horrible drum-based piece which usually gives you an instant headache and makes your whole body vibrate.

So the rule is, when driving in cities drive at your own pace, don't be bullied by anyone, watch out for signs, and if you get lost do what you can't do on a motorway – stop and ask for directions. Local pedestrians can be far friendlier than local drivers.

Dual carriageways

These are roads which have two lanes either side separated by a central reservation. Whenever I think of dual carriageways, for some reason I always think of the A303. This lies between

Hampshire and Devon, and is for the most part a beautiful road to use. I have used it thousands of times to get to the West Country, one of my favourite areas, and I know it well. It's divided into single-lane and dual carriageway sections, and in holiday seasons the single-lane bits can become unbearably slow.

This is a drawback of many dual carriageways: they're intermittently single-lane then dual carriageway, which can make drivers impatient – which is always a danger. There you are, stuck behind something or other, when, Praise the Lord, you suddenly see a 'dual carriageway ahead' sign and you know you're in for a bit of a burst. At this point everyone puts their foot down and tries to pass the slow vehicle at the front. However, at the end of the dual carriageway, as you

Did you know?

What happened to the M1 at Junction 3? The section of M1 from Junction 5 to the A406 North Circular Road was built over several years in the 1960s. It was constructed from Junctions 4 to 2 with the overpasses provided to add Junction 3 when the Scratchwood Link to the A1 had been built. However, the link road was cancelled in the end, leaving a redundant junction. Today, Scratchwood services (recently renamed London Gateway) occupies the site, and the incomplete roundabout has now become a set of slip roads for the approach to the services.

come towards another single lane section, it can be dangerous – you're desperate to overtake the remaining slower drivers so you try to get in front of them, often unaware that a car may be coming at you from the opposite direction at very high speed. I've reported many fatal accidents resulting from such scenarios, so would recommend that you always pull back as the dual carriageway becomes single-lane again, and do so in plenty of time. You may save your life.

B roads

'B roads' are numbered local routes, which have less traffic than main trunk roads. They are typically short, not usually more than 15 miles long. The classification has nothing to do with the width or quality of the physical road, and they range from wide roads like single-carriageway A roads, to roads barely wide enough for two cars to pass. They're often very picturesque, but danger can lurk around every corner. I have sideswiped a car on these narrow highways and it's true that in daylight it's often hard to see what's coming round the next bend. Always drive slowly along these little roads. They can be lethal.

Delays

If you do get stuck in a jam, try not to get stressed. I know this is easier said than done, but take some deep breaths, listen to calming music if possible and try to be philosophical. There really isn't anything you can do about it anyway.

If you're stuck in a queue behind an accident, spare a thought for the people involved. And if it's merely congestion, then believe that you're stuck there for a reason – that you're meant to be there. I promise: I've done it myself and it works.

I always keep stuff in the glovebox to keep me going, such as gum, pastilles and a soft drink, and I sing along with the radio or my favourite CDs at the top of my voice. That alone has been known to get the queues moving again. But stick something, anything, in your glovebox that will keep you sane. It's your call.

If you're travelling on motorways with kids or elderly people it's always worth taking extra water and sweets in case of long delays. Many, many times I've had calls from frustrated drivers who have been stuck for ages and need a drink. If the queue is particularly bad, local police will often supply water, but it can be slow to get through to you. Of course, that means a loo is likely to be needed too. You can buy small portable loos for cars now. They're great for kids, although I'm not sure I could relieve myself with a trucker peering down at me from his cab.

Rubber knickers

The Department of Transport states that 'inattention' is a factor in 25.8 per cent of all road accidents and 18 per cent of fatal accidents. This 'inattention' is also called rubber-necking, and is, I know, a huge source of frustration to drivers everywhere, but particularly on motorways. Rubber-neckers – or 'rubber knickers', as I once inaccurately called them on-air – cause massive delays. I don't actually blame drivers for this, because we're all inclined to ogle an accident, but it does, as the statistics show, cause further accidents on both sides of the road, as well as slowing down traffic. I'm frequently criticised for judging onlookers in a kind of 'for goodness sake don't do that' way. I never do, because, as I say, we are all inclined to do it. I simply report the traffic jams that result, which is, after all, my job.

Solutions for this are tricky. You can't exactly hide several mangled vehicles stuck on the hard shoulder, surrounded by fire engines, police and ambulances, so in a way it's hardly surprising that we have a look. Just try not to if possible. Concentrate on the cars immediately surrounding you, and that way you're far less likely to have an accident in the congestion that's built up in the area.

Hah Hah Hah!

A juggler, driving to his next performance,
was stopped by the police.
'What are those knives doing in your car?'
asked the officer.
'I juggle them in my act.'
'Oh yeah?' says the policeman. 'Let's see you do it.'
So the juggler starts juggling the knives.
'A man driving past sees this and says, 'Wow, am I
glad I've given up drinking. Look at the test they're
making you do now!'

The first ever motorway traffic jam was on a Bank Holiday weekend in early 1959, when thousands of motorists flocked to Lancashire to drive on the new M6. The 8.5-mile journey, that normally took eight minutes to complete, took well over an hour.

Hoggers

You know who you are. You are the drivers who insist on staying in the middle or outside lanes. You drive us all mad. There's a clear motorway ahead, and there you are, sitting in the middle lane, annoying the hell out of everyone coming up from behind, where we can clearly see the inside lane is empty. In fairness, I think we have all done it at some time, simply because the motorway *is* clear and we're lulled into a sense of ownership – this is *my* road, and I can drive *exactly* where I want! However, in more congested times it really affects the flow of traffic. The RAC has said that drivers who do this effectively 'steal' up to 700 miles of motorway during peak periods, which adds delays to everyone's journey. Not only that, but it can contribute to accidents as frustrated drivers try to get around them. Sometimes these middle-lane hoggers force other drivers to overtake on the inside lane, which is not only *illegal* but contributes to many accidents. It's worth remembering that the police are empowered to prosecute drivers for poor lane discipline if they think their driving is dangerous.

Operation Stack

If you're heading for either Dover or Felixstowe (most likely the latter if you're driving a container lorry), you could easily get caught up in Operation Stack. This normally happens when either the weather is bad and ferries are delayed, or if there's industrial action on either side of the Channel. Because of the large number of lorries that use these ports regularly, as soon as one of the ports is closed and delays start, traffic starts to back up incredibly quickly. In Kent, the police close the M20 coast-bound to 'stack' the lorries, in order not to block up the immediate area around the ports. Phase 1 involves closing the road between Junctions 11 and 12 near Folkestone, and Phase 2 involves closing it between Junctions 8 and 9 (Maidstone and Ashford). I've known the M20 to be closed for days, frustrating truckers and operators alike. Trucks just have to sit it out, but car drivers can use the old A20 alongside the motorway, although journey times are extended and many people may miss their sailings.

Felixstowe handles around 35 per cent of all cargo traffic, so if it's closed for any reason they have their own version of Operation Stack, which means lorries are parked on one lane of the Dock Spur Road to allow through traffic to pass. This is implemented when winds exceed 45mph, since the port's cranes cannot be operated due to Health and Safety regulations. Of course, this can happen quickly and can't always been foreseen, but if you're planning a

Did you know?

The first petrol gauge appeared in cars in 1922.

Did you know?

Traffic jams cost the UK economy an estimated £20 billion each year in lost productivity and deliveries. Not only this, but they increase pollution, and are a significant cause of stress.

shopping trip to France in December and the weather is bad, then check and check again before you leave the house. A good number to ring is 01394 604966 for Felixstowe Port information services.

... but don't forget your atlas ...

Chapter Seven

Sally's Driving Tips

'You never really learn to swear until you learn to drive.'
Anonymous

Planning a journey can make all the difference; no journey can be planned with 100 per cent accuracy because traffic conditions change from hour to hour – in fact from minute to minute – but with a bit of advance planning you'll arrive at your destination in good shape rather than bent out of shape.

I always think it's a good idea to plan an alternative route if you can for any journey, because things can and do go wrong. For example, if you suddenly hear of an accident or the weather changes, or roadworks suddenly appear, it's really good to have a Plan B. Many of the drivers who phone me at Radio 2 know the road network so well that when they hear of a blockage they immediately take diversionary measures, but inexperienced travellers should always plan ahead – it really is worth it. There's nothing worse than being stuck in an unexpected queue. It's not only frustrating, but it could be crucial to the outcome of your day. You might be late for an important interview, the start of a show, or an important date.

I never understand why anyone would spontaneously

Radio 2 is the biggest radio station in Europe, if not the world. 13.2 million listeners tune in every week, on FM alone. Tens of thousands listen across the globe via the internet.

hop into their car at five o'clock on a Friday night to set off on a long journey. This is a terrible idea. You will quickly become mired in miles of traffic. But people do! Then they ring me up and say 'Why am I stuck in a 20-mile queue on the M6?' Because it's *always* like that at 5:00pm on a Friday, that's why!

Most television stations now give out traffic information in the mornings, and some in the evenings. If you're travelling at these times just watch for a couple of minutes to see what's going on. There are now loads of websites that give out real-time traffic information too; they show you where roadworks are located, traffic hotspots and weather conditions, present and predicted. Such sites can be invaluable when planning an unfamiliar journey. See the appendix for some of the best.

Car things

It goes without saying that checking and double-checking your vehicle regularly is also worthwhile – oil, water, tyres, lights, electrics, brakes, and the security of roof racks and bike racks. If all these things are working and secure, then you'll feel a lot more confident as you set off! And if everything is in working order, you're much more likely to have a smooth journey.

R&R

If your journey is particularly long, make a note in advance of service stations and rest-stops along the way – the Highway Code recommends that you stop every two hours. I always carry a hotel guide in my car in case the weather turns bad and I need to stay somewhere urgently. There are many guides to hotels, truck-stops, B&Bs and hostels, and it really is worth investing in one and carrying it in the car at all times.

You should never start a journey when you're tired. I once set out from Penzance at eight o'clock at night, intending to drive all the way to London non-stop, but I only got about 80 miles up the road before I felt incredibly tired. It's particularly difficult to drive when you're tired and it's dark, when concentration is far more important. I thought that if I pulled into a lay-by along the way and slept for a couple of hours I'd be fine. But unless you're a trucker, with a lovely bed in a cab, sleeping in a vehicle is almost impossible. At least, it was for me. I really tried. In the end I found a nearby B&B and had a good sleep before continuing on my way.

Not only is it safer to start a journey refreshed, but it's safer for everyone else on the road too. Shockingly, government statistics show that one in five motorway accidents are caused by someone falling asleep at the wheel. In fact, according to Think!, the road safety organisation, an estimated 300 people are killed on our roads every year as a result of fatigue. Research commissioned by the Government found that if you fall asleep at the wheel you are 50 per cent more likely to die or suffer serious injury than in another road accident, because a sleeping driver doesn't react before a crash.

The greatest risk of falling asleep at the wheel occurs between midnight and 6:00am and between 2:00 and 4:00pm. Though people who drive as part of their job are generally more at risk, it can affect any driver.

And we're off

Once you're on the road it's difficult to know where the jams may be, but here are some tips:

Radio 2

I would say this, I know, but listen to Radio 2! We give the biggest overall picture of where the jams and problems are in the UK, but local radio stations are brilliant for problems in your immediate area.

Matrix signs

These are supposed to provide information about jams but are sometimes out of date. However, if you pass a matrix sign indicating a problem then it's wise to take it seriously and think about re-routing.

Roadworks

You'd be amazed at how many drivers *know* roadworks exist in a certain place, but nonetheless drive straight into them day after day! It happens to me too; it's been known for me to spend all day telling everyone about roadworks in a particular place, and then drive straight into them a couple of days later! It's easy to forget, but if you know there are roadworks on your route, just take a few minutes to look at a map and find a way around. It will save you time and money. It's true that roadworks won't necessarily hold you up, but problems arise if there's a breakdown or accident in the middle of them. In those circumstances your journey time could be doubled or even tripled.

Don't forget, SPECS (Speed Check Enforcement Systems) often operate in roadworks areas. This tracks you from the start to the finish of the roadworks, so you need to stick to the speed limit for the entire length. The cameras are yellow in colour and are signposted in advance.

Satellite navigation systems

These are becoming increasingly common and much more sophisticated. Some of them not only tell you the easiest way to get from A to Z but also warn you of roadworks and delays up ahead. I would be lost without such guidance. On one occasion I was likely to be late for a broadcast because of a terrible jam, but used my satnav to give me an alternative route and arrived in time for my first bulletin. I highly recommend them. If you are thinking of buying one of these systems, I'd also recommend you get one with an anti-theft device and mark it with your registration. In parts of the UK, police reports show that sat nav theft has risen by

Did you know?

In 1916, 55 per cent of the cars in the world were Model T Fords, a record that has never been beaten.

2,000 per cent in the last year and is now the number one reason for car break-ins.

However, don't think that satnavs can never go wrong. They can. There is the story of a coach driver on a school trip who used his satnav to guide him to Hampton Court Palace in south-west London. The kids from Orchard Lea Junior School in Fareham, Hampshire, were studying the Tudor period in History and were excited at the prospect of a day out at the Palace. So the driver punched Hampton Court into his system – and went on to spend all day driving in circles as the system directed him to Hampton Court, a small road in Islington, North London. He spent seven hours trying to find his way back to Hampton Court Palace but never made it. Apparently one of the kids managed to take a snap of the Houses of Parliament as the coach sped by, but that was all the history they got.

> **Did you know?**
>
> *The New York City Police Department used bicycles to pursue speeding motorists in 1898.*

So have a bit of an idea of your direction even if you have sat nav – the AA still advise keeping a map in the car at all times. Sounds like the coach driver could have done with one.

Quit while you're ahead!
Worst days to travel...

Of course, motorways and roads can become congested at almost anytime, anywhere, and queues are often unpredictable. However, here are a few general guidelines that have certainly proved true in my experience, and are backed up by research from the RAC and the Highways Agency:

- Friday afternoons attract more drivers to motorways than any other day, according to the latest research. This is also the day on which accidents are most likely to occur, particularly during the afternoon, with the peak number occurring at around 5:00pm.

- Motorways are generally busiest during afternoons, with Fridays being the worst. In particular, Fridays before half-terms, bank holidays and Christmas are awful. The Friday before the Autumn half-term is known as 'Black Friday', when congestion tends to increase by at least 40 per cent, with an additional 20 minutes on journey times across major routes compared to an average Friday.

- Friday morning is generally one of the best times to travel – until around 12:00 midday, that is, when the great exodus begins.

- Monday morning is the busiest time on every motorway in the country.

- August is widely regarded as the busiest motorway month.

- Sundays after 5:00pm are another time to avoid. Sunday is a great day for visiting, or simply driving somewhere for the hell of it. However, never set off to drive when you're feeling tired: Sunday lunch, followed by a heavy tea and a chat around a cosy fire, is wonderful, but it really can make you feel sleepy. According to the Highways Agency, 'Fatigue is the main cause of 10% of road accidents, increasing to 20% on motorways.'

- There's much less traffic on any day between midnight and 6:00am – but again, never, ever, drive if you're going to be tired.

If you travel in bad weather, particularly snow and rain, your journey time can double. This is partly because the accident rate rises at these times, creating longer queues and more congestion, but is also because poor conditions slow everything down. On 30 January 2003 thousands of drivers were trapped overnight in their vehicles on the M11 by heavy snow. Some abandoned their vehicles on the motorway and others were forced to drive the wrong way to escape. The problem arose because of a lack of gritting, which led to accidents, which then turned into huge tailbacks. Nowadays the Highways Agency have vastly improved their forecasting capabilities, and road gritting has become much more accurate. However, storms, snow and rain can be unpredictable and always increase journey times. I have personally spoken many times to listeners stuck in such conditions, and my advice is always the same: if conditions are truly awful, just stop and find somewhere to stay until it passes. Never worry about the expense; your lives are worth so much more than the cost of one night's accommodation.

Watch out for...

On some routes nowadays, the Highways Agency are trying out 'hard shoulder running'. This means that once a certain vehicle volume is reached on a road, an electronic sign appears above the hard shoulder indicating that it's open for use. However, if these signs revert to a red X it means that the hard shoulder has reverted to an 'emergency only' lane and goes out of use – in which case you should move back onto the main carriageway. Where such schemes exist the traffic flows much easier, and it really saves time.

There are also 'variable message signs' – signs above the road giving you up-to-the-minute information on changing conditions ahead. They also give out speed limit information, in the hope that if everyone sticks to the speed that's displayed everything will run at a steady flow.

If you start to feel sleepy at all, just stop and drink two cups of coffee, and allow some time for it to take effect before you start off again.

Don't have so much noise inside the car that you can't hear what's going on around you; music, kids, Playstations – they're all wonderful things, but don't let them get so loud that you risk not hearing a siren approaching, or a car horn.

> **Did you know?**
>
> *The automobile is the most recycled consumer product in the world today.*

A broad's abroad

This is a complicated area, since laws change from country to country and continent to continent. However, there are many publications and websites that can help professional and non-professional drivers alike. See the appendix at the back of this book.

If you plan to travel abroad regularly, it's well worth obtaining an IDP, or International Driving Permit, which, along with your UK licence, allows you to drive in other countries.

And lastly

I clearly remember a day when I was driving along the coast in Dorset. As I crossed the green hills, with the sea to my left, my hood down, staring at the sun, I suddenly remembered how wonderful driving could be. The daily grind of a commute, or the school run, or doing it for work, isn't romantic. But cars and journeys can still be wonderful, and can take you to places impossible to reach by any other means. With a bit of planning and preparation you can still enjoy places that will make your heart race with excitement. Try it.

Music for the Road

'I never listen to music in the house,
I listen to music in the car.'
Peter Tork of The Monkees

Ever since the early days of crackling long wave radio, music and the road have gone hand in hand. None of us nowadays can imagine driving anywhere without the radio or CD player helping us on our way. From the sweet abandon of a road trip to a summer's day driving with the top down, we all love to drive to music. And music for the road comes in all forms, whatever your taste, all of them creating a sense of freedom. And you can make your own music too. Many years ago, a girlfriend and I had a day out at the seaside, and on the way back we sang every Beatles song we could remember. The journey flew by.

In 1929, American Paul Galvin, the head of Galvin Manufacturing Corporation, invented the first car radio. In those days radios were not available from car makers 'as standard', and consumers had to purchase them separately. Galvin coined the name 'Motorola' for the company's new product, combining the idea of motion and radio. There's a bit of a debate about which was the first car to get a radio fitted as standard, but it's likely that it was a Mercedes in 1949; however, an all-transistor radio was offered for the first time on all 1955 Chrysler models.

In 1956 Chrysler actually manufactured a built-in record player and offered it as an extra on their cars: the 'Highway Hi-Fi Record Player' played special 16rpm EPs. In addition, in 1960 a record player fitted in Chryslers could play up to fourteen 45rpm records.

Top ten bands for top-down driving

1. The Eagles
2. Jimi Hendrix
3. Deep Purple
4. The Beatles
5. Fleetwood Mac
6. Led Zeppelin
7. The Who
8. Thin Lizzy
9. The Rolling Stones
10. The Beach Boys

Tracks I love to drive to

Born To Be Wild – Steppenwolf

King Of The Road – Roger Miller

24 Hours From Tulsa – Gene Pitney

Darling Be Home Soon – The Lovin' Spoonful

On The Road Again – Willie Nelson

Long Hard Ride – The Marshall Tucker Band

Wild Thing – The Troggs

Catch The Wind – Donovan

We Gotta Get Out Of This Place – The Animals

(Get Your Kicks On) Route 66 – Nat 'King' Cole Trio

Highwayman (Live) – Johnny Cash

Big Road Blues – Canned Heat

Lost Highway – Hank Williams

Road to Hell – Chris Rea

Truck Driving Song – Weird Al Yankovic

Coyote – Joni Mitchell
Traffic Jam – James Taylor
Walk This Way – Run DMC/Aerosmith
No Particular Place to Go – Chuck Berry

A classical music playlist for the road

Bach: Double Violin Concerto, BWV1043 – Vivace
Beethoven: Symphony No 5 – Allegro con brio
Delibes: Lakmé – Flower Duet
Elgar: Pomp and Circumstance
Elgar: Thomas Tallis
Handel: Sarabande (made famous by the
    Levi's TV commercial)
Handel: Water Music Suite No 1, No 3
Holst: The Planets – Jupiter, the bringer of Jollity
Mendelssohn: Violin Concerto in E minor –
    Allegro non troppo: Allegro molto vivace
Morricone: Gabriel's Oboe
Mozart: Symphony No 40 – Allegro Molto
Prokofiev: Romeo and Juliet – Montagues and Capulets
Rachmaninov: Rhapsody on a theme of Paganini –
    18th variation
Schubert: Piano Quintet 'Trout' – Theme and Variations
Tchaikovsky: The Nutcracker – Waltz of the Flowers
Verdi: La Traviata – Brindisi
Verdi: Rigoletto – La Donna è Mobile
Vivaldi: Four Seasons, Spring – Allegro

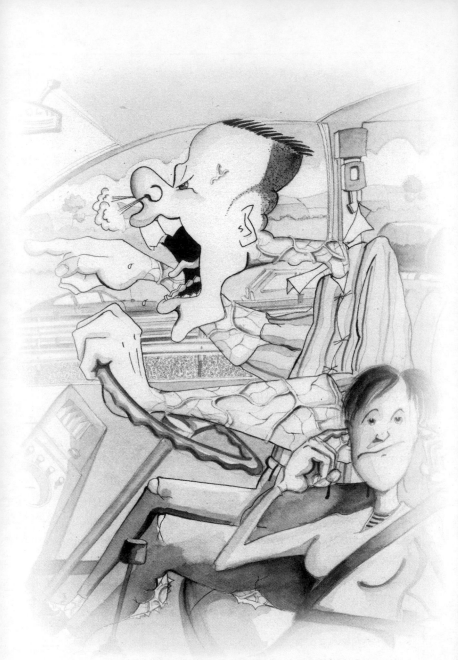

Calm down, calm down

Chapter Eight

Sally on Safety

> *'Safety is something that happens*
> *between your ears, not something you*
> *hold in your hands.'*
> Jeff Cooper

Do you realise, that statistically, motorways are the safest place to drive? In the latest Highways Agency research, only 3.9 per cent of the total number of accidents in the UK were on motorways.

However, accidents on motorways often have a bigger impact on congestion because there's no way of escaping. In order to help, the Highways Agency have introduced a system of traffic management called Incident Support Units, designed to take over some policing duties in the wake of a serious accident. In this way they hope to get traffic moving more quickly and thus reduce congestion. Nowadays it's quite common to see these units travelling up and down the UK's roads.

Remember that speeds are usually higher on motorways, so always leave a greater gap between vehicles than on other roads. At higher speeds stopping distances increase dramatically.

Motorway anxiety

A study by the RAC Foundation revealed that some motorists suffer from incredible anxiety when driving on a motorway. A third of drivers apparently admit to this condition, while 12 per cent will do anything to avoid motorways altogether. Some of the conditions experienced include raised heart rate and blood pressure, excessive sweating, tension headaches, stomach cramps, insomnia and digestive problems. These conditions were mostly found in young and old female drivers.

Drivers suffering from anxiety are much more likely to make mistakes, such as leaving indicators on, driving excessively slowly and 'tailgating' (driving too close to the car in front). It's likely that such drivers will also be hoggers, sitting in a road position that they're scared to move away from. So instead of getting angry when you come across them, try to be kind. They can't all be Michael Schumachers like you.

But if you really don't like motorways, don't use them. It's not a sin.

Breaking down

I once broke down on the M3 when I was very young and in my Hillman Imp. My instinct was to call my dad to come and get me, but the policeman on the end of the emergency telephone wouldn't let me. It was the first time I discovered that you always have to call an officially recognised breakdown service to get you off a motorway. Private recoveries can be very expensive, so it's a great argument for belonging to an official breakdown service.

If you do break down, move to the hard shoulder, with your wheels turned left away from the motorway. Put on your hazard lights, get out of your car, and move as far away from it as possible – up or down the embankment, or into the adjacent field – many accidents I've reported have involved other vehicles crashing into stationary vehicles on the hard shoulder, often with dire consequences. Never try to cross lanes to the other side of the motorway. That could cost you your life.

Rain

Rain is one of the most common and dangerous causes of all accidents. You're far more likely to be in a crash in heavy rain, and you'll almost certainly be delayed, because rainy conditions generally slow down the flow of traffic. But there will always be some idiot who drives through heavy rain at 100mph, and in my experience it's generally these drivers who end up in hospital, or worse. I always dread

Did you know?

Why do some motorways start at junctions numbered higher than 1? In all cases this is simply because the motorway was never built to its proposed length, usually because this would have involved taking it deep into a city, which would have proved problematic. Motorways which do this include the M23 (starting at Junction 7 outside London) and the M11 (starting at Junction 4 on the A406 North Circular Road, London).

rainy days at work, because I know I shall report many, many crashes.

Heavy rainfall on roads – particularly after a dry spell – is lethal: the road can become like an ice rink, and the excess of surface water greatly increases your chances of aquaplaning. Always drive especially slowly in such conditions, and if the rain is so heavy that you can't see, pull over somewhere safe, well off the road, and wait for it to pass.

Ice

It can take ten times longer to stop a vehicle in icy conditions, and many accidents I report are caused by drivers being unaware of this. If you do find yourself spinning on ice, get into a very low gear and let the car come to a natural halt, using the brake very gently. Never brake suddenly on ice. Black ice is particularly dangerous. This is transparent ice that looks black on top of the road surface; it can't be seen and can reach depths of two or three inches.

So the rule is: drive as slowly as possible when it's icy, and don't worry about the plonker behind you, tooting for you to go faster. Just get to your destination safely.

However, we should think ourselves lucky that we've never had to deal with ice in the way that the people of Toronto had to in March 2007. The city had suffered a severe snowstorm, which then turned to ice, large blocks of which – some measuring four by four feet – started falling off skyscrapers and crashing into cars. The police had to seal of the entire city until the danger had passed.

Fog

Always use dipped headlights in fog, and if you have a rear fog light, use that too – but always remember to switch it off after the fog clears! One of the most common complaints I hear from drivers is about fog lights left on in normal conditions; this can blind the driver behind you.

If it's very foggy, never be tempted to follow another car by hanging on to their tail lights. You can be closer to them than you think, making sudden braking very dangerous. And always remember: if it's terrible fog and you're nervous about continuing on your way, just pull off the road, stay overnight somewhere if you have to, and let someone know where you are.

Car crime

According to Home Office figures, vehicle crime has fallen by more than half since 1997. However, despite this there were still almost two million vehicle-related crimes between 2005 and 2006, so here is the Home Office's basic safety advice that may save you from becoming one of their statistics:

- Never leave items on display in your car. Anything at all can become a target, even something you don't think is valuable.
- Vehicle immobilisers are great. I've always had one fitted on every car I've ever had. These are simple devices which only let the engine come on when you've flicked a switch inside your car, which is usually hidden in a place that only you know. Most thieves wouldn't stop to search for it.

Immobilisers cost hardly anything, so go along to your local garage and get one fitted: they really are worth it.

- Always use a steering wheel lock when you leave the car unattended.
- Have an alarm system fitted.
- Always try to park in a well-lit, open space.
- Locking wheel nuts are cheap, easy to fit, and stop thieves from taking your wheels.
- Have your vehicle registration number or the last seven digits of your Vehicle Identification Number (VIN) etched onto all windows, windscreens and headlamps.
- Mark all equipment, such as the car stereo, with your vehicle registration number.
- Before buying a car, check whether it has been reported stolen or seriously damaged or is still subject to finance. It is up to you to make sure the vehicle you buy isn't stolen. If you do end up buying a stolen vehicle, you could lose all your money; lose the vehicle; inherit whatever problems the vehicle has (unpaid tickets, penalties etc); and risk the police taking an interest in your actions.

Safe not sorry

Always wear a seatbelt. These are a legal requirement and could save your life.

Don't tailgate. We've all had this experience, some plonker rushing up and sitting a few inches behind your rear bumper, so close that they can practically touch your briefcase, as it were. The Highways Agency says that there should be a gap of at least two seconds between vehicles, preferably four; otherwise if the vehicle in front brakes suddenly, there's bound to be a collision.

Never drive if you start to feel ill; and if you drive under the influence of illegal drugs or alcohol, you could face a ban, a fine of up to £5,000, or even a jail sentence. It's illegal to use a mobile phone when driving – using a phone increases

> **Did you know?**
>
> *In 1910, magician Harry Houdini was the first person to solo pilot a plane in Australia. He taught himself to drive a car just so he could drive out to the airfield – and he never drove again!*

the chances of an accident by up to four times. Always leave your voicemail on and check messages later. You could save your life, and other people's, by taking this simple rule on board.

Calm down, calm down

Road rage is on the up. For some reason, we live in an age in which many people feel they have a right to yell, scream and shout at anyone or anything that's hacking them off. Where have the courteous days of my dad's era gone? The days when the AA patrolman on his bike would salute any car proudly displaying an AA yellow and silver badge?

It may be to do with personal space, as roads become more and more crowded, or it might just be that we're turning into a nation of aggressive grouches. Whatever the reason, road rage takes it's toll on both the aggressor and the victim.

Both end up distressed and far more likely to have an accident, both during and after the incident.

I can't say I've never yelled at someone, given them a Victory sign, or cursed as I passed. I have. But then we all have, and it never, ever, makes us feel better. It just cranks up the blood pressure and the adrenalin levels, making it harder to focus on the important thing – which is driving safely.

A recent Gallup poll showed that more than 80 per cent of drivers have experienced some form of road rage. But initiatives like www.roadrage.co.uk have started to provide a real forum to fight against road rage, and not to shout back.

So the golden rule is: if someone starts, ignore it, and never *ever* get out of your car to confront another driver; you don't know what they have in their glovebox, and they may assault you. If someone annoys you, then try and be forgiving. I know, I know. They've nearly just killed you, and you want revenge. But you've survived, and whatever happened may not have been deliberate. I once went into a rage because someone behind me on a motorway was continually flashing – and no, I wasn't in the middle lane. I just thought he was being an arse, but it turned out one of my rear lights was about to fall off and he was just being helpful.

Even if someone is deliberately aggressive, let them get on with it. Move out of their way and *never* respond to their hostility. Stay safe inside the car, and when the incident is over, just take it easy. If you're really shaken up, stop when it's safe, and calm down. Try and have some calming music in the car at all times. This is an ideal time to play it.

It's the limit

Here is the Highway Code Speed Limit table as a useful guide:

	Built-up areas	Elsewhere	
		Single carriageways	*Dual carriageways*
Type of vehicle	**mph**	**mph**	**mph**
Cars and motorcycles	30	60	70
Cars towing caravans or trailers	30	50	60
Buses and coaches	30	50	60
Goods vehicles *(up to 7.5 tonnes laden weight)*	30	50	60
Goods vehicles *(above 7.5 tonnes)*	30	40	50

Smile – you're on camera!

We love them and we hate them – the debate about speed cameras rages on. I was amazed to find that Britain's first conviction for speeding was in August 1959, when a driver was caught speeding in Lancashire and was fined a total of £3. This seems to have begun a trend, and now it's very much the norm to get caught for speeding on roads throughout Britain.

I've amassed points like most of us nowadays, and I've argued against the unfairness of it all. But what all those points have done is make me drive slower generally. Once, I was a bit of a girl racer, but now I know better.

In my youth I lived for a while in Bermuda, where there was a blanket speed limit of 20mph across the whole island. One of my most frightening experiences ever was coming back to the UK after being there for two years and jumping into a car to drive up the M23 and M25 to London. I felt as if I was on an horrific fairground ride, with everything whizzing past at this enormous speed. The thing is, we get used to driving dangerously without even realising it. And the more we get used to it, the faster we go. Remember – the cameras are there to tame you!

The speed camera debate

This debate divides and inflames opinion. Some people see it as a tax-raising exercise, whilst others genuinely believe that reducing speeds literally saves lives. Although road fatalities have reduced since the introduction of the cameras in 1995, some argue that the reduction is too small to justify the amount of money raised through the cameras, which now number over 6,000 throughout the country. And the number is growing.

However, the arguments are complex. Some motoring associations claim that if you're driving along an empty road at 50mph at three o'clock in the morning, you're far less dangerous than someone driving past a busy school in the morning *within* the speed limit, say, of 30mph.

Camera stats

- A 2006 study found that nearly a million drivers are approaching a ban thanks to points racked up through speed cameras (*The Scotsman* 9 March 2006).
- Speed traps can make six figure sums each month (Sky News 20 April 2005).
- A Mori survey in 2003 found that seven out of ten motorists accepted that cameras reduced crashes, saved lives, and made motorists slow down (BBC News).
- The equivalent of one in every five drivers have been caught for speeding since 1996 – that's seven million prosecutions… (speedcameras.org).

When tragedy strikes

Whenever I report an accident, I'm always aware that behind that glib phrase there lurks misery and devastation for many people. I too have personal experience of such tragedies, and the resulting pain never really leaves you. The general trend in fatal motor accidents, though, has declined since the early 1990s, mainly due to more driver awareness, more safety features on roads, and ever more safety-conscious cars.

However, any road death leaves behind it untold heartache. The judicial system in general is seen to be lenient on drivers who kill, further adding to the pain of loss.

In the 1960s, road deaths in the UK peaked at nearly 8,000 per year. Since then they have fallen steadily, to less than half that number. Since, over the same period, the amount of traffic on the roads (that is, the total number of miles travelled by motor vehicles) has trebled, the actual improvement is clearly even greater.

Sweden has one of the best road safety records of any country in Europe. One of the ways that they've achieved this is by virtually separating pedestrians from any cars that travel at more than 30mph. They have also improved facilities for pedestrians and cyclists, and have extremely strict rules for anyone caught driving under the influence of either alcohol or drugs. And not surprisingly, the reduction of alcohol and drugs limits for drivers has been accompanied by a fall in casualties.

There are several great support services around to help families and friends who have been affected by a road death: SCARD, standing for Support and Care after Road Death and Injury, is one of these. Mandy Roberts, one of its founding trustees, helped start the organisation after her daughter was killed. The organisation now helps with all aspects of road accidents, including legal and educational issues. They help steer relatives through what is probably the most traumatic time of their lives, when nothing can prepare them for the legal and emotional maze with which they're confronted. With an average of 3,500 road deaths a year, the organisation has its work cut out. Although police forces have been relatively successful in kerbing some drink-driving, accidents which happen under the influence of recreational drugs are on the increase.

'My dream is that one day we won't be needed at all,' says Mandy. 'I guess the biggest success story for me has been myself. If it weren't for the formation of SCARD ten years ago, I wouldn't be here today. My daughter was an only child, and when she died I had absolutely no reason to carry on living. There was no way out. With SCARD, I realised that there could be a life afterwards. I now have a young family. It doesn't change what happened, but it gave me a reason to keep getting up in the morning.'

Mandy is one of thousands of relatives affected by reckless driving. It's a sobering thought that it could happen to any one of us. I hope you never need it, but their website address is www.scard.org.uk.

My hero

Chapter Nine

Knights of the Road

*'There is more credit and satisfaction in
being a first-rate truck driver than
a tenth-rate executive.'*
B.C. Forbes, *founder of* Forbes Magazine

Without trucks, and those who drive them, all of our lives would grind to a halt. They aren't known as the 'Knights of the Road' for nothing.

Road-freight transport has evolved from the wagons and stagecoaches of the 16th century to the high-tech vehicles that we see on our roads today. At the start of this evolution, large wagons of maybe two to four tons' capacity were drawn by as many as six horses or oxen, but by the First World War trucks had begun to develop into the vehicles we know today. Being a truck driver then, though, required muscle power and endurance. Most trucks didn't even have a cab, and drivers sat on an uncomfortable wooden seat on the outside of the truck, exposed to the elements.

As we've seen, roads were not the smooth tarmac things we know today either. They were often full of potholes and difficult to negotiate. The average working day for a trucker was tough. According to research done by truck manufacturer

Scania, an average haulier worked up to 3,800 hours a year, compared with today's average of about 1,700 hours.

Today's drivers are spoilt in comparison, sitting as they do in climate-controlled cabs, in contact with the world via advanced satellite technology. Still, no matter how much people communicate by e-mail and mobile phones, travel on fast jet aircraft and expect instant service, most goods are still being hauled the 'old-fashioned' way: by road.

Trucking seems to me to be a culture and lifestyle like no other. Drivers spend hours every day, alone, with just their truck and possibly the radio to keep them company. One of the reasons I think that I have a great relationship with them is because we're together for a lot of the day, and in some ways our relationship is a bit like a marriage: I try to be supportive and helpful, and, of course, love them in my own way. But then, we can have arguments. If I tell them something that isn't true, they phone up and have a go.

Did you know?

The longest distance between motorway junctions is westbound on the M26 from Junction 2A. The next interchange is with the M25, but exiting there isn't possible in this direction. The next exit from the motorway is some 18 miles later, at M25 Junction 6. Signs on the M26 warn drivers of this. A close runner-up is the M11 southbound from Junction 10: Junction 9 is limited access, leaving a 17-mile non-stop journey to Junction 8.

Sometimes I shout back, but if I make a mistake then, just like a marriage, I usually apologise, and then they feel bad. So we make up, and we start all over again.

The fact of the matter is, we have a fundamental understanding and respect for what each of us does. When I started out I felt that I wanted to help drivers who, day after day, do a job that most of the population take for granted, and that most people really wouldn't want to do. It's stressful, tiring, and sometimes thankless. Of course, this feeling extends to all sorts of other drivers too; coach drivers, in particular, do an amazing job of ferrying us around the country, and even commuters travelling the same road with boring regularity need a friend. But truckers who listen to Radio 2 are very loyal. They usually listen all day, every day, and they are an incredibly important community to the station.

Of course, they aren't all perfect. Like any group of drivers, they make mistakes, and because they drive all day their stress levels are usually much higher than others'. They have to meet sometimes impossible deadlines, and they work in an environment that is polluted, noisy and dangerous. If you combine a mentally stressful situation with a physically demanding one, then the chances of becoming ill are much higher than in many other jobs. But you won't often hear them moaning. The majority of truckers love their jobs, and almost all of them have hearts as big as their trucks. Just remember to keep those hearts healthy: eat right and exercise when you can. I don't want you leaving me just yet, thanks.

CB radio

Although the idea of having a radio link between two or more people was first introduced into the United Kingdom from the US in the 1970s, it remained technically illegal for many years. The Government only finally caved in and legalised it in November 1981, although at that time a licence was still required to own and operate a CB or 'citizens' band' system. This last legal requirement wasn't lifted until December 2000, by which time CB had become a standard form of communication, particularly between truck drivers. This was, of course, in the days before mobile phones, the widespread use of which has resulted in CB usage declining somewhat.

However, CB has escaped the legislation that now applies to mobile phones. In other words, it's not illegal to use CB whilst on the move. For this reason some truckers still use it as a way of transmitting information between themselves, to warn of delays and other such things.

Even when they no longer use CB, a lot of the callers to Radio 2 still use their old CB 'handles', or names. It's always a pleasure to talk to Crazy Horse, Snowman, Blue Fox, the Badger, the Wizard, Cameo Dodger, Yorkie... the list is endless. But these names always reflect an aspect of the driver's personality, so are extraordinarily personal and special. If I get it wrong, or if another driver uses a name already in use, I can get my ears burnt, let me tell you.

CB also has a language all of its own. When I get calls from truckers, some still leave messages in CB-talk, so I've become familiar with it over the years. Some examples are:

Let's eyeball – Let's meet.

How many candles are you burning? – How old are you?

Do you copy? – Can you hear me?

Roger – Yes.

Smokey – Police car.

Bear – Policeman.

Bear in the air – Police helicopter.

Bear in the bushes – Police hiding.

Beaver – Woman.

Brush your teeth and comb your hair – Watch out for speed traps.

Return journey – Flip flop.

Knocking at your back door – Someone is behind you.

Eighteen-wheeler – Articulated lorry.

Breaker Breaker – I want to start transmitting.

Hah Hah Hah!

A policeman pulled a car over and strolled up to the driver's window: 'Excuse me sir, but do you know that you're driving without a rear light?'
The driver jumped out and ran to the rear of his car and let out a whimpering groan. The driver seemed so genuinely distressed that the policeman took a sympathetic view:
'Don't take it so hard, it's not all that serious...'
'Isn't it?' the driver cried.
'Where's my caravan gone?'

So they might say, for instance: 'Breaker Breaker, brush you teeth and comb your hair there's a bear in the bushes.' (Hello, just warning you of a speed trap ahead where police are hiding off the road.) Or: 'Breaker Breaker, how do you fancy an eyeball on the flip flop, beaver?' (Would be lovely to meet you when I come back, lady.)

As the craze became more popular in the UK, even places got their own nicknames. For instance, London became Noddy Town; Cardiff was Smokey Dragon; Northwich was Salt City; East Kilbride was Polo Mint City (because of its abundance of roundabouts) and so on.

Another way to communicate in CB uses the '10' code. Each ten is followed by another number, and each has a separate meaning, thus:

10-1 – Receiving poorly

10-2 – Receiving well

10-3 – Stop transmitting

10-4 – OK, message received

10-5 – Relay message

10-6 – Busy, stand by

10-7 – Out of service, leaving air

10-8 – In service, subject to call

10-9 – Repeat message

10-10 – Transmission completed, standing by

10-11 – Talking too rapidly

10-12 – Visitors present

10-13 – Advise weather/road conditions

10-16 – Make pick up at…

10-17 – Urgent business

10-18 – Anything for us?

10-19 – Nothing for you, return to base

10-20 – My location is...

10-21 – Call by telephone

10-22 – Report in person to...

10-23 – Stand by

10-24 – Completed last assignment

10-25 – Can you contact...

10-26 – Disregard last information

10-27 – I am moving to channel...

10-28 – Identify your station

10-29 – Time is up for contact

10-30 – Does not conform to FCC (a US body) rules

10-32 – I will give you a radio check

10-33 – Emergency traffic

10-34 – Trouble at this station

10-35 – Confidential information

10-36 – Correct time is...

10-37 – Wrecker needed at...

10-38 – Ambulance needed at...

10-39 – Your message delivered

10-41 – Please turn to channel...

10-42 – Traffic accident at...

10-43 – Traffic tie up at...

10-44 – Have a message for you

10-45 – All units within range please report

10-50 – Break channel

10-60 – What is next message number?

10-62 – Unable to copy, use phone

10-63 – Net directed to...

10-64 – Net clear

10-65 – Awaiting your next message/assignment

10-67 – All units comply

10-70 – Fire at...

10-71 – Proceed with transmission in sequence

10-77 – Negative contact

10-81 – Reserve hotel room for...

10-82 – Reserve room for...

10-84 – My telephone number is...

10-85 – My address is...

10-91 – Talk closer to the mike

10-93 – Check my frequency on this channel

10-94 – Please give me a long count

10-99 – Mission completed, all units secure

10-200 – Police needed at...

Lady truckers

The first lady trucker on record was Lillie Elizabeth Drennan, an American, born in 1897. After a couple of marriages and a stint as a telephone operator, she started a trucking company with her husband in 1928, and she got her truck driving licence the following year. She had to endure prejudice from a then all-male profession, but proved herself by winning many safety awards, and winning

Did you know?

Buick introduced the first electric turn signals in 1938.

competitions. She became known throughout the industry for her tough persona, and was instrumental in recruiting other female truckers during the Second World War. She eventually became a popular media personality, and really did pave the way for all women hauliers, both in the US and around the world. Nowadays women truckers are more commonplace, although just 2 per cent of Britain's 400,000 truckers are female. Many of these wonderful women telephone into Radio 2, and seem to love their free-wheeling lifestyle. You go, gals.

Truckers abroad

Many of you will know someone who drives abroad regularly. Over the past few years some UK truck drivers have been arrested, and sometimes even imprisoned, for carrying illegal items, from people to drugs. We're used to being treated fairly here in the UK, but legal systems abroad are different; there, you're guilty until proven innocent, and the judicial process can take some time. Many European countries arrest and imprison drivers in a matter of hours or days, with no chance of a fair trial, and no access to proper legal representation.

In 2002 the House of Commons launched an enquiry into the issue of truckers imprisoned abroad, and concluded that at that time, there were up to 100 Dutch and 19 British drivers in jail across Europe, with a further 26 British drivers on remand. Statistics for the number of drivers held at any one time are hard to get, because prisons rarely release the occupations of inmates. But many are held all across Europe, often unfairly, until their sentence has been completed. Authorities in France are particularly unforgiving, and a report by Dutchman J.B. Vallenduuk, a solicitor in Haarlem, Netherlands, into the treatment of Dutch drivers arrested abroad concluded that France is one of the countries most guilty of unfair treatment of drivers.

One driver I spoke to was stopped by customs officials in France on a Saturday afternoon, and by 11am on the following Tuesday had been convicted and sentenced to two years in prison. By any standards, this could be seen as rough justice. When he appealed his sentence, they added an extra year, making it a three-year stretch. Fair Trials Abroad did their best to represent him, but it came to nothing. He was finally released 18 months into his sentence. Guilty or not, European Law says that the driver of the vehicle is ultimately responsible for the load, no matter what the circumstances.

If you are planning to work abroad, *always* check and double check your load as thoroughly as you can. It may save a traumatic experience.

Truck safety

Road-freight crime is on the increase. These crimes come in all forms, from hijacking whole loads to stealing the truck or simply nicking the diesel or stuff from inside the truck. According to uk-trucking.net, almost half of such crimes are committed because ignition keys have been left in the truck, so *always* remember to take your keys out, no matter how safe you think you are. There are now many 'safe parking' areas for trucks across the UK, and it's always worth checking that if your drive involves an overnight stop, you can find somewhere safe to park.

TruckPol, founded in 2003, was set up specifically to fight freight crime across the country. I have been personally involved with West Midlands Police, who actively promote safe truckstops and the prevention of freight crime in general across their region, and other regions also have police units dedicated to the reduction of this area of crime. They are aware that some freight crime is perpetrated by organised gangs, who prey on truckers and their loads across the country.

A list of safe parking areas, and other tips, can be found in the *Highways Agency Truck Stop Guide*. Don't forget – it's free!

Did you know?

The steepest motorway hill is the Northern Ireland M2 climbing away from Belfast between Junctions 2 and 4. It reaches a gradient of 1 in 15 at one point (the recommended maximum is 1 in 25). The only uncertainty is that no figures are available for the gradient of the M90 between Kinross and Perth, which is the only route with the potential to beat this incline. Niall Wallace has attempted to survey it using Ordnance Survey maps and has arrived at the figure of 1 in 10 between the Bridge of Earn and the top of the hill. That's very steep indeed!

You probably know it anyway, but...

Some good advice for truckers:

- Always make sure you check your load; even if you didn't pack it, it's still your responsibility.
- If you're carrying a hazardous load, you can only stop at a recognised truck stop.
- Make sure you know your weight limit.
- Make sure you know the height and width of your vehicle. All bridges below 16ft 16in (5m 3cm) must, by law, show their height so that you can pass through safely; but remember, that limit applies only to the width of the white lines, or 'goal posts', displayed on the bridge.
- Double-check that any ropes, straps and curtains are tight and secure enough to withstand braking
- If your vehicle is over 9ft 10in (3m) tall then you have to display the exact height in the cab, in order to avoid any guesswork!
- If you do misjudge and strike a bridge, the authorities will look to recover the costs of vehicle recovery and any other damage. Don't ever hit and run. The consequences of leaving the scene are severe.
- Some tunnels and bridges have extra restrictions for high vehicles and hazardous loads in bad weather and overnight.
- Fuel theft is a growing problem, so always check your fuel pipes haven't been tampered with before setting off after parking up.
- Diesel spills can cause accidents and delays, so, in order to avoid them, don't overfill your tank, and make sure your

fuel cap is fastened securely. Also check that the seal isn't torn, worn or missing.

- Plan ahead with your finances; remember to manage your day properly by taking money for tolls etc. and always keep a paper and pen to make a note of expenses.

You can get a FREE copy of the *Truck Stop Guide*, published by the Highways Agency, by either calling 08701 226 236 or logging on to www.heavygoodvehicle.com.

Remember...

They deliver everything from food to clothes to car spares to animals to fuel – and more. They are on the road night and day, getting your supplies to the shops where you'll eventually buy them. Some have been driving for over 40 years – one of my callers is named Million Mile Man, because he's now driven beyond that staggering figure. So when you see these men and women trundling about the roads of the UK, spare them a thought and give them a break. Though like any group of human beings they're not 100 per cent perfect, they come pretty darned close, and I love them.

Life on the road

This is how some truckers feel about their life and work:

Richard Joy from Selby, who drives for LiftTrans UK:
'I've been a trucker for ten years. My dad and brother are lorry drivers, and I fancied having a go. It definitely runs in the blood. I used to go with my dad when I was four or five, and my son does the

same now. He loves it. When the weather's nice, it's glorious, although when it's bad it's a miserable job. But being in the countryside is a joy.'

Dickie Halstead from Leeds, who drives for Scoby and Mackintosh:

'I've been at trucker for 27 years. My dad got me into it, and it runs in the blood. Rules change, but I wouldn't say it's more difficult these days – you just have to get on with it. I love the freedom of being out on the road. Anything's better than being in work.'

Famous truck drivers

Boris Karloff – truck driver and asphalt spreader before becoming a monster.

Sean Connery – worked as a trucker before spying took over.

Brad Pitt – a limo driver before becoming a limo passenger.

Elvis Presley – his first job after school was as a trucker; his dad also drove trucks for a living.

Matthew McConaughey – worked as a trucker, amongst other things, before driving all of us women mad.

Johnnie Walker
and me on a day out
with Scania.

Being interviewed in the Peterborough Truckfest arena.

Bob Limming (left) and Colin Ward from Truckfest. They've just seen the takings for the day.

Trying to drive a Heavy Goods Vehicle and look glamorous at the same time (Steve Barber)

Doing my Queen wave at Truckfest.

BRISTOL
(01454)
777 887

SUREWAY

Me and Bonnie Raitt – the most amazing woman. I loved her.

A picture of 'my' Eddie Stobart truck (Sally B). This was auctioned off for Children in Need.

Voted 4th most attractive voice on radio! I was honoured to be in such legendary company.

EDDIE STOBART LTD
EXPRESS ROAD HAULAGE SPECIALIST

STOBART

"Sally B" - Heading Home
by Robert Tomlin

Sally B

6 Stephanie Hughes

6 John Inverdale

4 Sally Boazman

3 Brian Perkins

4 John Peel

3 Natalie Wheen

Penny Gore

Radio Times 26 January–1 February 2002

Johnnie Walker, James Taylor and me. You can tell James loves and adores me!

Presented to Sally Boazman with sincere thanks
for helping us with our project from
Buccaneer Distributions

28

The daily grind and
talking with my
hands as usual.

The Big Girl with
the Big Man from
the Big Show
(Day Macaskill)

Err...just a couple of
points, Sal......
(Day Macaskill)

We love you Sally but . . .

Chapter Ten

Crufts for Trucks

'Trucks in general keep me coming back –
they're in my blood...in my system. I like seeing
the new trucks, and it's a good meeting point.'
Eric Thomas from Holyhead

If you listen regularly to Radio 2, you'll know that one of my favourite pastimes every year is attending Truckfests. There are many of these across the country, some of which I have never attended, but I know from talking to truckers how popular and essential they are, wherever they are. They usually involve prizes for the best presented trucks in all different classes, while, just as important, also giving truckers a chance to meet and mingle with their colleagues; driving can be a solitary job, so these social and competitive events are vital to the industry.

I attend about half-a-dozen every year, and it's a great chance for me to meet a lot of the drivers who regularly phone in to Radio 2, and to thank them personally for all their help during the year. They're wonderful events, bringing together not only truck drivers from all across Europe, but their families too. It's a great chance to get together and talk about all sorts of things – not just trucks, but the haulage industry in general – and to see hundreds of trucks in all their glory. And they *are* glorious to behold: big, beautiful, bold, and wonderfully looked after by very proud owners. One of the highlights of the festivals are the competitions; there are all sorts of classes and divisions, and the trucks entered are polished and honed to perfection.

The Truckfests I go to are run by Colin Ward and Bob Limming, who first met in 1978, when Colin was an events organiser and met Bob at a massive fireworks display where he'd been hired to organise the lighting. They instantly hit it off. After several ventures, including running a talent agency, they were asked by Austin Rover to run a special hospitality day at Donington Park. Although car-based, the organisers wanted trucks along too, and as these magnificent beasts started rolling in to the event, they realised that trucks really should have a show all of their own. They saw that cars and trucks had plenty of places to be displayed together, at events across the country, but after talking to truckers realised that those who drove and operated these vehicles hardly ever got to go along to such events themselves; their bosses did, but they never thought to take their employees. It was time for them to have an event of their own.

Bob and Colin wanted to plan an event that was not only for truckers but for their families too. Some drivers spend

Did you know?

British Petroleum makes a profit of £3,800 per second!

long hours away from their wives and kids every week, and they saw it as a great chance for such families to spend some time together, away from the daily grind of driving up and down the country.

Their first ever Truckfest was held at the Newark Showground, near Peterborough, in 1982. They had no real idea of how to publicise this one-off event, so they came up with the idea of sitting in a car at the side of the road, night after night, transmitting details via CB radio of how wonderful this up-coming event would be. Of course, news quickly spread, and with this first step in what's now called 'gorilla marketing' they were off.

They had risked everything to make this first unique festival work. All their money was on the line, and they knew that if no one turned up it would be a disaster. Though the event was held at Easter, it snowed heavily the night before, so the omens were not good. 'We woke up that morning and thought "God, we're dead ducks!"' says Bob. But suddenly all the roads around the showground were blocked with traffic trying to get in. The Newark and Nottinghamshire police were going crackers trying to get all the trucks off the M1, and at that moment, says Bob, 'we knew we'd done it.'

This Truckfest was the first of many. In 2007 the festival celebrated its 25th anniversary and there are now six held annually across the country. The crowds are always enormous. But ask any truck driver where the home of the Truckfest is and they will always say Peterborough, in the centre of the country, on the A1. But wherever they're held, and whoever they're held by, such events create a real sense of belonging to a community, a wonderful community, where drivers can exchange stories, introduce their families to each other, gossip and, of course, enter competitions.

But they're vital for other reasons too. It's here that truckers find their voices, talk to other members of the haulage industry and display a real sense of pride in their work. Think of the Oscars, the Baftas, the MTV awards. Well, Truckfest is the professional truck drivers' equivalent. When a prize is won, tears are shed, reputations are made, and the applause is loud and sincere. According to Bob, Brian Wetherley from Commercial Motors has described the event as 'An image booster for the whole industry.'

I once witnessed the Eddie Stobart Fleet – 90 trucks in all – lined up, with all their drivers wearing their famous ties and shirts. Other fleets enter the arena polished to perfection, shining with pride. This sense of pride, displayed not only by the drivers themselves but also by their colleagues, is something to behold and it can bring tears to my eyes. It makes me very proud to be associated with each and every one of them.

Haulage companies have learned to cherish their drivers because, sadly, it's a profession that no longer attracts people in the great numbers it once did. But to some extent things have changed. The old greasy image of the truck driver of the past has changed as the Eddie Stobarts, William Morrisons and Earlhams of the industry have come to realise that customers want to see a smart driver and truck turning up at their businesses. This image, together with the hi-tech nature of modern trucks, means that truck driving has become much more of a real profession. Truckfests reflect this, and have themselves changed with the times. The appeal of these events

Did you know?

On average there's about 3,000ft (980m) of electrical wiring in every car.

themselves, though, endures regardless of trends.

It's at these festivals that you'll see trucks beautifully painted with all kinds of scenes. The rise in popularity of painted trucks is also partly due to Colin and Bob – they had seen some at a truck festival in France, and were so taken by the beauty of these machines that they decided to bring them across, en masse, to one of the shows. The lavishly ornate vehicles were an instant hit, and British drivers started to imitate them. Of course, artwork on transport has a long and varied history, and played an important part even in the days of barges and horse-drawn wagons. The artwork on lorries covers many subjects, including current events and celebrities, and can be quite stunning.

I try and meet as many drivers as possible whenever I attend a festival. I know most of the exhibitors by name, and some truckers are at all the events, every year, and we are now like old friends. But my appearances haven't always gone to plan. At Truckfest in Edinburgh one year, the Scottish Truckers Club, run by the wonderful Dougie, put me on their stage to sing a song with their compère. The song we sang was *Blanket on the Ground*, and halfway through it the compère dragged me to the floor just as we got to the main line, to demonstrate that we were, really, lying on the ground. As he did this a hairpiece I was wearing dislodged itself, and I crawled off-stage hanging on to what was left of my hair to fix it in the wings. But there was no mirror, so I did the best I could. Returning to the stage I was greeted by jeers and laughter because I'd put it on back to front! I looked ridiculous.

The first time I went to the festival at Haydock Park near Liverpool, I went with Johnnie Walker. The roads into the showground became so jammed that the police had to seal many of them off in the surrounding area. Once in the ground we were surrounded by no less than 12 security guards, because the crowds were so enormous. This had never happened to me before, or since, so I guess it was the Johnnie Walker factor!

Of course, there are always celebrities far more famous than me at these events – lots of soap stars, and TV stars in general. Colin and Bob have managed to lure the likes of Take That (with Robbie!), Richard Hammond, Noel Edmonds, Michael Barrymore...the list is endless. Bob and Colin's wives, Penny and Daphne, still remember making breakfast for Take That on the day of their appearance. The band were so popular that they eventually had to be smuggled out of the ground in an ambulance for their own safety. I've never, by the way, had that problem.

I have a particular soft spot for Jim Bowen, who, like me, has made many appearances at the festival, and who sometimes travels round with me during the show. He never stops making me laugh and is a true gent. The crowds love him to pieces, and I'm proud to say he's become a friend. Richard Hammond and I have also done the rounds as a duo. He's always struck me as a truly talented man, funny and charming, so along with the rest of the country I was horrified when he had his accident in September 2006, and thrilled when he pulled through. When we met up at Radio 2 some months later, I greeted him with outstretched arms and said 'You're still alive!' to which he replied 'Only just!' One year Eddie the Eagle was invited, although he turned up two hours late and wearing his slippers!

The devotion that truckers have to this festival can sometimes be astounding. The organisers were once contacted by a solicitor in Nottingham who said that one of his clients, a trucker, had asked for his ashes to be spread across the showground in Peterborough. The organisers were honoured to arrange it. There have been marriages, births, the lot. One year there was a bomb scare at one of the grounds, and the police had to evacuate the whole area. Or try to. One regular was sitting in the Grandstand with his sandwiches when the police came along to remove him. He wouldn't budge. He simply said 'I come here every year, I bring my picnic, I make sure I'm the first in the gate, and

> **Did you know?**
>
> *The first drive-in cinema was opened in Camden, New Jersey, in 1933; and the first drive-in bank was opened in Los Angeles in 1937.*

Did you know?

In 2007, a study carried out by EuroRAP found that the A682 between Junction 13 of the M65 and Long Preston in Lancashire was the most dangerous road in the UK. It was the only road to feature in the report's 'higher risk' category. Nearly 100 people have been killed on this stretch in the last decade, and its record of fatalities and injuries is ten times that of other roads.

this is the seat that I like. I've been coming here since it started and I'm not moving for you or anyone.'

I have been attending Bob and Colin's Truckfests every year since 1999, and so feel very much part of the family and the community. Unknowingly, I've continued a tradition with Radio 2 connections: the first ever celebrity to attend the Newark Truckfest back in 1982 was Sheila Tracey, who was then hosting an overnight show on the station. She had built up a fantastic rapport with truckers who worked on the roads through the night, and they loved her. So she was invited to that very first show, and I feel proud to be following in her footsteps.

You may have gathered by now that I think Truckfests, and the people involved with them, are fantastic. They really reflect the whole industry, and give it a boost like no other event, so there's nothing else like them. Long may they continue.

Thoughts on Truckfest

This is what some of the truckers think of Truckfest at Peterborough:

Frank Digman from Cambridgeshire, who drives for D.C. Morris:

'This is the second time I've shown a truck, and it's been fantastic. I reckon we'll get a "highly recommended"…that'll do us! It's all about the people. Everyone's having a good laugh and enjoying themselves. The stalls and shows are good…suddenly an old mate will bang on your back door!'

Dave Betts from Peterborough, who drives for P.C. Howard:
'It's all about the atmosphere – it's like a big family.'

Another re-mortgage on the way

Chapter Eleven

The Beleaguered Driver

*'The tax collector must love poor people – he's
creating so many of them.'*
Bill Vaughn

Governments come and go, but motorists always seem to
be at the sharp end of their thinking.

Car tax

Vehicle taxation started with the turnpike roads: as they
were privately built, the owners demanded, and got, a
payment from everyone who used them. This included riders
on horseback and passengers in carriages and coaches. In
1637 Hackney carriages were taxed for the first time, and at
the same time a system of licensing was brought in for them.
Over a hundred years later, in 1747, any carriage drawn by
two or more horses incurred a tax and licence too. In 1861
the Locomotive Act decided that any steam-powered vehicle
and any horse-drawn carriage should be subject to tax,
although the local authorities who administered these taxes
only allowed for travel within their immediate area: a
further tax was required if you dared to venture into the

The Peanuts characters were first animated in 1957 for a Ford Falcon automobile commercial.

next council's land. So even then the taxman had you by the throat. The steam-powered vehicles were often large and cumbersome, and could severely damage the road surface, so the Government of the day felt justified in getting them to help pay for repairs.

In the early 1900s the Motor Car Act was passed, specifically designed for the increasing number of cars then appearing on the roads. It required all vehicles to be registered and licensed annually, and fines were introduced for drivers without registration. The registration fee was £1 (or 20 shillings) for a car and five shillings for a motorcycle. Local authorities were made responsible for collecting the tax, and remained so until the formation of the DVLA in Swansea in 1974. In this early period the car tax was determined by the size of the engine: this was calculated at £1 to 1hp, and was rounded up to the next pound for anything bigger. Later the RAC rating of tax was introduced. The Finance Acts of 1909 and 1910 stated that funds raised through this tax were to go directly towards maintaining and constructing roads. At least you knew where your money was going in those days!

Since then car tax has risen sharply and, most recently, the Government is trying to encourage drivers to be greener by taxing vehicles accordingly. This is controversial to some owners, who feel they are being penalised for choosing a particular type of vehicle (usually a 4x4), and say that a higher tax on these vehicles infringes on their civil liberties.

Fuel tax

Duty on petrol was introduced into the UK in 1909. Then, it cost 3d (just over 1p) on top of the price of a gallon of petrol, which was about £1. Around 1921 it was abolished altogether as the price of petrol rocketed, and its removal caused prices to fall steeply. However, prices rose steadily again over the next 70 years, and in 1993 the Government introduced the Fuel Price Escalator, which automatically added tax to the price of fuel, ahead of inflation. It was argued by the Government that this action could stem the tide of pollution and car use in general, and thus lead to less emissions. This ran until 2000, when protests across the UK demanded a reduction. The end of the escalator was announced in November 2000, at which time fuel in the UK was the most expensive in Europe. In 1993 it had been amongst the cheapest.

Cambridge Econometrics have calculated that by abandoning the escalator, four million extra tons of carbon emissions have been freed into the atmosphere and 11 per cent more fuel has been consumed than would otherwise have been.

> **Did you know?**
>
> *The city with the most Rolls-Royces per capita is Hong Kong.*

Congestion charging

Although this is only operating in two cities in the UK at present, it's introduction to other cities seems inevitable. At present, anyone driving into London between the hours of 7:00am and 6:00pm, Monday to Friday, is charged £8. Driving into Durham will cost you £2 between 10:00am and 4:00pm Monday to Saturday.

Did you know?

Most American car horns beep in the key of F.

If you add car insurance, the maintenance cost of your vehicle and possible parking fines, the final sum for just owning and driving a vehicle can be staggering. And you pay all of this money and *still* get stuck in queues that sometimes stretch for miles. Catch the train, they say. Save your money. If only that were possible...

Friday!

Chapter Twelve

And Finally...

*'I'm a prisoner of the white lines
and the freeway...'*
Joni Mitchell

Traffic reporting isn't rocket science. The world wouldn't stop turning if we all gave up, and many people think it's not an important job at all. Indeed, most people could do it, but the perception that it's a really easy job isn't entirely true. First and foremost you need access to a great stream of information, and to know what's important and what isn't. And then you need to explain it all to people who are usually really fed up and have been stuck somewhere for hours, and let them know you're on their side. Being a driver yourself is important too, because otherwise it's not possible to understand how frustrating losing hours of your life can be. Believe it or not, I heard of one radio station that employed a traffic reporter who *didn't* drive, and I couldn't understand why. If you can't empathise with the horror of driving into a jam then it's not possible to be passionate or understanding about your work.

Although some now famous celebrities started out as traffic reporters (and are usually embarrassed to admit it), I've never seen the job as a stepping-stone to something else. I know that's the sole reason why some people do the job at all. I love to have fun and banter with the presenters, but that's never more important than the information. So I continue to see it as a worthwhile job in its own right, like any other kind of reporting.

By Friday I'm frazzled, but not as frazzled as the truckers and commuters who've been on the road for hours all week. So I get the best end of the deal.

I know from experience that people who say traffic reporting is a waste of radio time are those who don't drive a lot. They've told me as much. There are others who say that you can never give a decent national traffic report, because local traffic news is all we need. This is true if you just drive locally, but for drivers who travel the length and breadth of the country every day a much more comprehensive picture is helpful. If you're setting out to Birmingham from Glasgow, for example, it's useful to know if the M6 is blocked in Cumbria, because then you can use another route.

I can guarantee that we'll all get stuck in a jam

Did you know?

Computerised warning signs first appeared on motorways along the Severn Bridge section of the M4 in June 1968. This system was introduced at the London end of the motorway in 1969.

sometime, and when we do we'll want to know how long the queue is, how long we'll be stuck in it, and how come we didn't know about it in the first place. Some callers phone in to Radio 2 and ask why I've mentioned every jam in the country except theirs. That's because when we do find ourselves delayed, we automatically think that the jam we're in is the most important. And for you it is. Then, suddenly, the traffic news is very important indeed.

I usually have a stream of Radio 2 colleagues either popping in to see me or phoning me on a Friday afternoon, telling me that they're going away for the weekend, and asking what's the best route to take. Are there roadworks along this bit of road? Would you say that this road is better than that road? Will we arrive at our idyllic weekend retreat frazzled or calm? Indeed, will we get there at all? The thing is, traffic really does affect most people at some time in their lives, so to get it right as often as possible is incredibly important.

It's never possible to keep everyone happy, and the worst aspect of the job is knowing you might be letting someone down by not mentioning a queue you don't know about. When drivers ring in to complain that I haven't mentioned their queue, I simply say that, talented as I may or may not be, I haven't yet devised a way of flying over the motorway system to view queues and make notes whilst simultaneously broadcasting from Central London. I rely on information from many sources, some of which are better than others, but they don't always tell me everything – it's not an infallible system. What I can always rely on are the Radio 2 listeners, and for that I am always grateful.

Driving is still as exciting to me as it was when I first drove Esmeralda all those years ago, and it can still be exhilarating discovering new places only accessible by car. I have driven thousands of miles over many years, and although it's not as trouble-free as it once was – with our crowded roads and the ever-increasing cost – it's still, for me, the best way to travel. You're free to go whenever you like, control how fast you travel, and listen to beautiful music at the same time. Cars today are better than ever, sturdier and safer, and nearly everybody has one. But whether you have a Ferrari or an ancient wreck like my first car Esmeralda, take the time, once in a while, to enjoy the experience. And be safe.

Acknowledgements

Anyone who's ever attempted to write a book knows that although it's mostly solitary work, help and support along the way is vital.

So my thanks go to my agent, June Ford-Crush, who persuaded me to write it in the first place, and whose support throughout the process has been unwavering.

My editors Derek Smith and Mark Hughes at Haynes Publishing have also steered me through the maze of putting a book together, and they have always done so with incredible patience and understanding.

I am also grateful to Nic Philps who helped with some of the initial research, and to my friends and family who helped to recall some early memories, and understood why I locked myself away for weeks on end.

Many, many people have contributed stories and information in the pages that follow. Too many to mention by name, but to all of you, I extend my thanks and gratitude.

Finally, thanks to the Radio Two listeners who continue to help me in my job day after day, and have contributed immeasurably to the contents of this book.

Sally Traffic's Ultimate Quiz

So you think you know it all? Here are some questions that will test your knowledge to the limit – check at the end to see how good a driver you really are...some of the answers are in the book, others you just have to know. Don't cheat, but the answers are at the end!

1. What is the UK's longest motorway?

_____

2. How old do you have to be to obtain a full driver's licence?

_____

3. How much is the toll for a car at the Dartford Crossing on the M25 motorway?

_____

4. What year did Sally Traffic start at Radio 2?

_____

5. Name the town off Junctions 15 and 16 of the M6 motorway.

_____

6. Where does the M1 start and finish?

_____

7. What was the name of the man who first thought of illuminating road crossings?

---

8. When is the worst time to travel?

---

9. Name three counties in the UK with no motorways at all.

---

10. How much is the daily congestion charge in London?

---

11. Which other town, apart from London, operates a congestion charge?

---

12. What is the speed restriction for a lorry over 7.5 tons on a single-lane carriageway?

---

13. In CB language, what's a 'smokey'?

---

14. What's the name of the system for parking lorries in Dover when the ferries are delayed?

---

15. Is the total mileage of motorways in Britain:

    a) 2,201.88 miles (3,544km)

    b) 2,516.5 miles (4,050km)

    c) 4,745 miles (7,636km)

16. What is the most expensive motorway built in the UK so far?

17. Where was the first motorway service station built in the UK?

18. According to Government statistics, which is the busiest stretch of motorway in the UK?

19. How much do you have to pay at the tolls when you leave Wales?

20. Which publisher's books were used in building the M6 toll road?

Answers

1. The M6 motorway, which is 230 miles long.
2. 17.
3. £3.
4. 1998.
5. Stoke.
6. Starts at Brent Cross, London (Junction 1), finishes at Leeds East (Junction 48).
7. Leslie Hore-Belisha (1895–1957), the Minister of Transport who introduced them in 1934.
8. Any Friday afternoon.
9. See the list on page 73.
10. Currently £8, as of 20 May 2007.

11. Durham.
12. 40mph.
13. A policeman.
14. Operation Stack.
15. a) 2,201.88 miles (3,544km).
16. The M25.
17. Watford Gap, between Junctions 16 and 17 of the M1 motorway.
18. The western section of the M25, between Junctions 12 and 16.
19. You don't – it's free.
20. Mills and Boon.

Reference Section

Websites to check before you set out on a journey

The Highways Agency – www.realtime-traffic.info
AA Traffic Watch –
www.theaa.com/travelwatch/travel_news.jsp
Get Me There –
www.getmethere.co.uk/telematics/index.html
RAF Traffic Info – http://www.rac.co.uk
Traffic Map – http://www.trafficmap.co.uk
Vauxhall TrafficNet – www.vauxhall.co.uk/vx/
    travelandleisure/trafficnet.do?method=loadTrafficNet
Trafficmaster – www.trafficmaster.co.uk

Websites to check if you plan to travel abroad

Driving Abroad – www.drivingabroad.co.uk
Driving Abroad – www.driving-abroad.info
Drive Alive – www.drive-alive.co.uk/driving_tips.html
The AA: European Driving –
www.theaa.com/motoring_advice/overseas/index.html

Sources for this book

www.dft.gov.uk/pgr/statistics/datatablespublications/
   tsgb/2005edition/transportstatisticsgreatbritain2005
www.highways.gov.uk/know
www.bbc.co.uk
www.wikipedia.org
www.cbrd.co.uk
www.PatheticMotorways.com
www.bumperart.com
www.funny2.com/bumper.htm
www.ruighaver.net/bumperstickers/index.htm
www.stickergiant.com
www.comedy-zone.net/jokes/laugh/transport/index.htm
www.jokes2go.com
http://fun.twilightwap.com/jokes.asp?joke_cat=
   RoadsandDriving

The Guinness Book of Records